LIKE NOBODY'S WATCHING

Crown House Publishing Limited
www.crownhouse.co.uk

First published by
Crown House Publishing
Crown Buildings, Bancyfelin, Carmarthen, Wales, SA33 5ND, UK
www.crownhouse.co.uk

and

Crown House Publishing Company LLC
PO Box 2223, Williston, VT 05495, USA
www.crownhousepublishing.com

First published 2019. Reprinted 2020.

British Library of Cataloguing-in-Publication Data
A catalogue entry for this book is available from the British Library.

LCCN 2019945825

Print ISBN 978-178583399-1
Mobi ISBN 978-178583453-0
ePub ISBN 978-178583454-7
ePDF ISBN 978-178583455-4

Printed in the UK by
TJ International, Padstow, Cornwall

ACKNOWLEDGEMENTS

I am very lucky to work at Heathfield Community College, East Sussex: a school that fosters a culture of professional trust and encourages its teachers to seize their agency, become more informed and teach like nobody's watching. I would like to thank our senior leadership team for their role in creating this culture and especially our head teacher, Caroline Barlow, for her support, advice and guidance over the years.

I would also like to acknowledge my colleagues from across the wider profession and especially those found on Twitter who have been generous in their sharing of words of wisdom.

Finally, I'd like to thank my wife, Zoe, for her help and support. Her passion for teaching and improving the life chances of children permeates this book.

CONTENTS

INTRODUCTION

THREE BELIEFS: THE SIMPLE, THE COMPLEX AND THE COMPLICATIONS

This book is based on three things that I believe to be true. Firstly, that teaching is, at its heart, simple. If you want to teach someone something - whether it is how to drive, bake a cake or understand the evidence for plate tectonics - you start by reminding them of what they already know (recap), you then tell or show them something new (input), you direct them to apply and practise with the new concept (application) and then you give feedback on how they are doing. Simple.

The second thing I hold to be true is that doing these simple things well is complex. There are many ways to remind pupils of what they know and even more ways to introduce them to something new. It is this complexity that makes the job of teaching so endlessly fascinating. It is also why it is a profession that requires a high level of training and continuous reflection and development of its members.

My third belief is that teaching has become overcomplicated. Teachers have endured decades of competing and conflicting advice about how they should teach, and spent an inordinate amount of time trying to please outside observers. In my career to date, I have been instructed to do all of the following:

- Test pupils to determine their learning style and plan different activities so pupils could choose one that matched their style.
- Start the lesson with Brain Gym activities. Stop the lesson frequently to do more Brain Gym activities.
- Plan every hour-long lesson as a three-part composition of starter, activity and plenary.

- Not talk for more than 10% of the lesson in total.
- Let pupils discover knowledge for themselves.
- Mark work every two weeks. Use one particular colour pen. Have pupils respond in a second colour. Respond to their response in a third colour.
- Base all learning objectives on Bloom's taxonomy and aim for the higher-order thinking skills in each lesson. Have pupils write every objective in their books.
- Don't teach subject knowledge, as pupils will always be able to look that up. Instead, focus on teaching transferable skills - like evaluation or creativity.

These complications have moved us a long way from the simplicity of recap, input, application and feedback, and have made teaching less effective. They have also added to our workload by making teaching less efficient.

FADS: WHERE GOOD IDEAS GO TO DIE

Many of these complications arise when good ideas about how to approach the simplicity of teaching well (i.e. the complexities) are turned into strategies and then passed on to teachers as policies. As I mentioned, there are many ways of delivering the input of new information. One way that became popular (certainly when I started teaching in 2003 and still frequently recommended to teachers on discussion forums today) was a carousel task in which pupils would take turns to visit a table to read the sources of information on it before moving on to the next. This was seen as preferable to simply giving them the information where they sat.

It is entirely possible that somewhere within this strategy there was a kernel of a good idea: a rationale that helped to explain why it was being done and how it was meant to improve learning. If there ever was, it was quickly lost. It became something that teachers were told they should be doing in their classrooms. It was imposed on them, divorced of its underlying explanation. It became a fad.

Sadly, we can see too many good ideas rapidly turn into fads:

- **Knowledge organisers** could be a powerful tool for departmental planning and for self-quizzing, or they could be a task given to already overburdened teachers for them to create and forget about.
- **Retrieval quizzes** could be a useful way to start the lesson and help pupils to make links between different parts of the subject, or they could be a random selection of questions chosen because someone has been told that lessons should begin with a quiz.
- **Growth mindset** sounds like a sensible principle. We want pupils to believe that they can achieve. This could involve carefully scaffolding tasks so that they taste success and know what they are aiming for, or it could be communicated via an assembly and a poster.
- **A knowledge-rich curriculum** could involve a deep understanding of what our subjects entail, with a thoughtful approach to the substantive and disciplinary thinking behind it, or it could involve making a list of what you think pupils should know for the exam.
- **Chalk and talk** could once again be seen as the bedrock of the lesson, whereby an expert carefully unpicks the subject with the use of analogies, diagrams, modelling and questioning, or it could involve someone talking incoherently for 20 minutes and then saying, "Now answer the question."

All of these ideas, amongst many others, will appear in this book. What I hope to do, though, is to explore the *why* (the theory underpinning the practice) as well as the *what* (the practice itself). In this way, we can act as professionals and choose how to apply the principles of effective teaching in our own classrooms. This enables us to have the confidence to teach like nobody's watching.

WHAT DOES IT MEAN TO "TEACH LIKE NOBODY'S WATCHING"?

When I talk about teaching like nobody's watching, I mean teaching the way you would naturally if left alone to get on with it. Teaching in this way demands confidence, and this confidence comes from having a good understanding of what works. Whilst this develops with exposure and practice, we also have to remember that our own experience can sometimes be a poor guide to what is most effective.[1] This is where a knowledge of educational research can prove invaluable. It acts as a guide and as a check to what we believe to be true.

This body of research (covering everything from how pupils learn to how teachers can develop themselves) also helps us to untangle the web of misinformation and contradictory advice that many of us have been given since we first started teaching. It can show us that it isn't the case that pupils remember only 10% of what they are told but 90% of what they teach others; that group work isn't necessarily better than individual work; and that differentiating objectives is unlikely to be effective.

These discussions always raise the knotty question of whether there is a "best" way to teach. I'd suggest that there is, but only if we keep the terms very loose. If we accept that:

- "teach" means to ensure that pupils know, understand and can do what we think they should know, understand and be able to do
- "way" means an approach, and
- "best", in this context, means most effective and efficient

then we have the question, "Is there a most effective and efficient approach to making sure pupils know, understand and can do?"

This book has the twin pillars of *effective* and *efficient* at its heart and these two terms need some unpicking. "Effective" is perhaps less controversial. When we talk about something being effective, we simply mean that it works. Hitting a nail in with the butt of screwdriver might be just as effective as using a hammer. Both get the

1 See David Didau, *What If Everything You Knew About Education Was Wrong?* (Carmarthen: Crown House Publishing, 2015).

job done. Likewise, there are many effective ways to teach. We can, as we will discuss, make almost anything work.

Bringing the term "efficient" into education tends to raise more eyebrows. Efficiency tends to mean doing something with the fewest possible resources. At a time when school budgets have been slashed in real terms and everyone is trying to do more with less, it is understandable that the word efficiency causes some alarm. It gets used to justify everything from larger class sizes to firing teaching assistants (TAs).[2] In this context though, I mean something slightly different. I mean efficiency in terms of our own personal resources: our time and energy as teachers.

This book will seek to answer the question of how to teach like nobody's watching by looking at how we can modify our practice in a way that is not only efficient in reducing workload but also effective at creating cultures of excellence from the classroom up.

We ignore this point about efficiency at our peril. Teaching can be an immersive job and it will fill any time you allot to it; the job is never really finished. This creates two significant problems:

1. **Burnout.** There is a serious UK-wide issue with both teacher recruitment and teacher retention, with an increasing number of teachers leaving the profession each year.[3] In many cases this is driven by an unsustainable workload. If we want to keep teachers in the job, we need to make the job efficient.
2. **Opportunity cost.** There are many things we could do that might make a difference to our pupils. However, time is finite. If we spend time doing one thing because we believe it is important, we have less left over to do something else that might be even more important.

---

2 See for example the Education Endowment Foundation (EEF) Teaching and Learning Toolkit, which shows the cost and impact of any given type of intervention. TAs are listed at a high cost with only one additional month of progress and reducing class size is also expensive for only a three-month lift in progress. The toolkit is available at: https://educationendowmentfoundation.org.uk/evidence-summaries/teaching-learning-toolkit.

3 Will Hazel, Reasons to worry: 5 new facts about teacher retention, *TES* (27 September 2018). Available at: https://www.tes.com/news/reasons-worry-5-new-facts-about-teacher-retention.

I would argue that one of the biggest problems in schools up and down the country isn't a lack of effectiveness (we are good at making things work), but a lack of efficiency. We are often instructed to do things in a way that takes more time to get the same result. This wouldn't happen if we taught like nobody was watching. Then we would find the most efficient way.

Professor Daniel Muijs, head of research at Ofsted, likens this to being instructed to eat soup with a fork.[4] If someone asked teachers to do this, we would try. Not only would we try, we would find a way to make it work. The soup would get eaten but at what cost? There would be a lot of mess, a lot of frustration and a lot of time wasted. This book suggests that teachers should instead bring along their own spoon.

HOW TO USE THIS BOOK

I believe that an excellent education starts with excellent individual teachers and that in recent years there has been too much of a focus on school structures as a way of driving improvement. The layout of this book reflects that approach and puts the emphasis very much on what each teacher can do to make a difference in their own classroom.

Part I will consider the individual lesson and discuss how we can build lessons around four simple elements:

1. recap
2. input
3. application
4. feedback

Each chapter will consider one aspect of the lesson in turn and discuss its importance – with a particular focus on how educational research can be applied to it in

4 Daniel Muijs, Keynote address at the researchEd Durrington conference, Durrington High School (28 April 2018).

the classroom, how it might look in different subjects, and the potential pitfalls to avoid.

Part II recognises that lessons don't happen in isolation but as part of a wider curriculum. This section will discuss:

- The creation of a programme of study that takes pupils on a journey through your subject.
- The super-curriculum of what happens outside the classroom.
- The principles of assessment design.
- How time in departments can be used to reduce workload and support a culture of excellence.

In Part III we will look at the role of the wider school in supporting teachers to teach like nobody's watching and how leaders can help to set them free from some of the more burdensome pressures.

I hope that this book will be a practical, and essential, guide to effective and efficient teaching and will give you the confidence to relax into your role and teach like nobody's watching.

PART I
THE LESSON

INTRODUCTION TO PART I

In most schools, it is in the lesson where the individual teacher has the most control, or at least it should be. Unfortunately, many schools have weighed teachers down with long lists of non-negotiables that they are expected to demonstrate in their classrooms. These demands are loaded with various myths about learning that have lingered from teacher training or from years of poor continuing professional development (CPD). The problem has also been driven by fear and a culture of high-stakes accountability. This has led to pedagogy in the classroom being shaped around an idea of what Ofsted are looking for.[1] This, as we shall discuss throughout this book, distorts our practice by asking us to teach for outside observers and not for our pupils.

Part I takes a look at the lesson and asks, "What would the lesson look like if teachers took back control of their own classrooms?" To answer this question, we will have to take a good hard look at a number of sacred cows in teaching – for example:

- Testing is neutral and doesn't lead to learning.
- Pupils benefit from written comments on their work.
- We should plan engaging activities.

1 See, for example, Daisy Christodoulou, *Seven Myths About Education* (Abingdon: Routledge, 2014).

- Noisy classrooms are a sign of learning.
- Teachers should limit how much they talk.
- Pupils need to discover knowledge for themselves.

There is one point that we need to discuss before we get started:

- Teachers need to plan lessons.

As with many myths in education, this seems too self-evident to be challenged, but challenge it we must. For as long as I can remember, the hour-long lesson has been king. When we train to teach, we are required to complete plans for each of the hour-long lessons we will deliver, with clearly defined objectives that will be met at the end of this unit of time. In many schools, the requirement to create lesson plans for each hour is still there, especially for observed lessons. This hour-long lesson should invariably involve some sort of starter, then a task or series of tasks, and then a plenary to demonstrate what has been learnt. Even if we aren't writing out individual lesson plans, this way of thinking about a lesson is still engrained from our training. But it is wrong.

Whatever made us think that every objective can be met in exactly one hour? Or, magically, in 50 minutes if that is how long the lesson is? Some things must take more time to learn than others and yet we still think of learning as having to fit into neat blocks of time that begin when pupils enter the classroom and end when they leave.

Before we can do anything else, we need to stop planning lessons as hour-long blocks of time and start thinking about planning learning. When I talk about a lesson comprising of four elements - recap, input, application and feedback - I don't mean to suggest that these should be worked through in the hour. Rather, whilst meeting an objective, over however long, all four elements should be present. This might involve recap at various points, a mix of input and application, and time for feedback throughout. It might take ten minutes to meet an objective or five hours.

CHAPTER 1

RECAP

FROM THE CHALKFACE

When I started teaching, we had hour-long lessons, in theory. In practice we had 40-minute lessons because the start and end were devoted to starters and plenaries. We were explicitly told that the start of the lesson need not have anything to do with the topic of the rest of the lesson, and should be used to "engage the class" and get them excited. Apparently, the idea that the lesson itself could be engaging didn't cross anyone's mind. This led to hours of work as I tried to devise exciting and engaging little starters. Pupils would roam the classroom looking for clues about today's objective, come in to the sounds of tropical rainforests and imagine what it would be like to sail down a river, or be given cards which each revealed one piece of information and have to search for someone with a card that related to it. It took ages, no one learnt anything, and it would take them time to settle down again afterwards.

Now I usually start with a quiz.

WHY DO WE START THE LESSON WITH A RECAP?

I am lucky enough to have the opportunity to see a lot of teachers teach. I wander in and out of classrooms in my own school and sometimes get invited to do the same in other schools. Wherever I am, and whatever subject I am observing, I almost always hear the same words towards the start of a lesson: "Last lesson we …"

"Last lesson we ..." is the teacher equivalent of "Once upon a time" or "In a galaxy far, far away". It indicates that the lesson is underway, that we have begun. And it isn't only in the classroom that we find this. When I was learning to drive, I remember each lesson beginning with a quick reminder of the basics learnt last time. When learning to bake I made an apple crumble, and that lesson started with a reminder that rubbing in the fat and flour was the same method we'd used with the scones we'd made the week before. When we are teaching something, we naturally start with a recap of what went before.

To recap is to "recapitulate" - to go through and summarise the main points of a previous meeting or document. It is literally a step backwards. So why does learning start in this way? Shouldn't we be starting our lesson by rushing headlong into a new learning objective? Isn't going back over something you have already done a bit boring?

Let us look at each of those concerns in turn.

Why does learning start with recap?

I would suggest that there is a reason why so many lessons, in and out of the classroom, start with the magic words "Last lesson we ..." It is because it works. Humans are natural teachers and intuitively know how to pass on what they know to the next generation. In *Making Kids Cleverer,* David Didau cites research from psychologists who looked at young children who were teaching each other to play board games and deployed the same kind of strategies as trained teachers. This leads to him concluding:

> this is somewhat alarming as it suggests that much of what teacher training and professional development consists of are competencies possessed by the average 5-year-old![1]

As we shall see, learning doesn't just occur from the study of new material, but from the constant recollection of material we have studied before. If we don't revisit

1 David Didau, *Making Kids Cleverer: A Manifesto for Closing the Advantage Gap* (Carmarthen: Crown House Publishing, 2019), pp. 51–52.

something, we struggle to remember it. The adage "use it or lose it" seems to apply here. Teachers, and possibly 5-year-olds, instinctively understand this.

Shouldn't we start by moving straight on to the next objective?

This is certainly how I was encouraged to start a lesson when I began teaching. We were told that a lesson should begin with something to excite the pupils about what they were going to learn, which would engage them in the lesson. Whilst this is well intentioned, it runs the risk of each (albeit very exciting) lesson appearing to be a distinct silo of information. This doesn't allow complex schemas to develop (as we will explore shortly).

Isn't going back over something you have already done boring?

Short answer: no.

Having the chance to use what you have learnt is far from boring. It gives pupils a feeling of progress and a way of actually seeing what they have learnt. We also need to keep in mind that our perspective of the school day is very different to that of our pupils. When they leave our classroom, they don't exist in a vacuum. They will have learnt new things in half a dozen or so other subjects, and will have done various other things outside of school as well. Spending a few minutes to pause and reflect on what they have already learnt can be an important break from a bombardment of new information.

As with everything else that we do, it is important that we are clear on the function we want recap to play in our lessons. Barak Rosenshine, in his seminal paper Principles of instruction, suggests that teachers start their lesson with a review of previous learning for two reasons:[2]

1. To practise recalling previously learnt material, thereby strengthening the ability to recall it in the future.
2. To link new material to that which has come before.

---

2 Barak Rosenshine, Principles of instruction: research-based strategies that all teachers should know, *American Educator* 36(1) (2012): 12–19, 39. Available at: https://www.aft.org/sites/default/files/periodicals/Rosenshine.pdf.

This chapter will consider how retrieval practice leads to more secure learning and the importance of developing schemas, and then explore what these two things look like in the classroom. We will finish by looking at some of the potential pitfalls to avoid.

THE PURPOSE OF RETRIEVAL PRACTICE

We would like to think that pupils leave our lessons having learnt something. Indeed, a huge amount of time and energy is expended by teachers in trying to demonstrate to outside observers that this has happened. One problem with trying to demonstrate learning is that the word itself is so hazily defined. Jeffrey Karpicke and Phillip Grimaldi provide the rather neat definition that "learning represents the ability to use past experiences in the service of the present."[3] To say that something is learnt means that a person can use information from one point in time in another, and in a different context. If a pupil is taught to recognise the verbs in a particular piece of writing, we would expect them to be able to recognise verbs in a different piece of writing before we could say that they have learnt to recognise verbs.

Karpicke and Grimaldi argue that this has some important implications for teachers. They suggest that in the past, learning has been associated with study - with the acquisition, encoding or constructing of new knowledge. And so we have a culture of doing, in which the activity is king in the learning process. This has meant that the act of retrieval has been regarded as a way of testing that this learning has taken place. The retrieval itself was seen as a neutral act that had no impact on learning. Weighing the pig did not make it grow.

Research in cognitive science, however, turns this culture of doing on its head and shows that it is not the studying of material that leads to secure learning, but the retrieval of it - recalling it back to mind. When we do this, we don't just replay what we have learnt but instead have to reconstruct it in light of new information and in a new context. This idea is not new. It was discussed by Hermann Ebbinghaus in the late 19th century, and he noted that whilst memory of a subject faded over time,

3 Jeffrey D. Karpicke and Phillip J. Grimaldi, Retrieval-based learning: a perspective for enhancing meaningful learning, *Educational Psychology Review* 24 (2012): 401–418 at 401.

every time it was recalled the memory lasted longer.[4] His work has been replicated and refined since and the principle is now widely accepted.[5]

It is the interplay between the working memory and the long-term memory that makes recap so important and so useful. Our long-term memory is almost limitless in its capacity to store information. Our working memory, however, can hold very little at any one time: this is why it is so difficult to remember a phone number someone leaves on an answerphone message and you find yourself having to chant it to yourself over and over again as you search for a pen. Once the number is in your long-term memory, though, you can access it with ease and without even noticing that you are doing it.

This also helps to explain why a phone number like 106621 is easier to remember than 439721. The number 1066 already has a meaning in your long-term memory. Those four numbers are chunked together as one piece of information. You therefore only have to remember three things: 1066 and 2 and 1.

When we talk about retrieval practice, we need to be very clear about what we mean. It doesn't mean simply going back over something (recap more generally); it is about actively trying to recall something from our long-term memory. This means that retrieval practice needs to be done without access to notes on the subject. Simply revisiting a topic isn't retrieval because we are effectively outsourcing our long-term memory to the resource that we are studying. And restudying is not as effective as retrieving.

Henry Roediger and Jeffrey Karpicke's research compared the effects of studying with those of retrieval.[6] They created three experimental groups of pupils who read brief scientific texts under different conditions:

1 The first group read and studied the text in four study periods.
2 The second group read and studied the text in three periods and tried to recall as much as they could in the fourth period.

4 Hermann Ebbinghaus, *Memory: A Contribution to Experimental Psychology*, trs Henry A. Ruger and Clara E. Bussenius (New York: Teachers College, Columbia University, 1913 [1885]).
5 Jaap J. M. Murre and Joeri Dros, Replication and analysis of Ebbinghaus' forgetting curve, *PLoS ONE* 10(7) (2015): e0120644. Available at: https://doi.org/10.1371/journal.pone.0120644.
6 Henry L. Roediger, III and Jeffrey D. Karpicke, Test-enhanced learning: taking memory tests improves long-term retention, *Psychological Science* 17(3) (2006): 249–255.

3 The third group studied the text in the first period and spent the next three periods trying to recall as much as they could.

Despite receiving no feedback on the accuracy of their recall, the third group of pupils who focused on retrieval far outperformed the ones who focused on repeated study. This point about feedback is picked up in a paper by Butler and Roediger, who found that although retrieval without feedback still produced positive effects, tests with feedback were even more effective.[7] Perhaps more surprising was their finding that this positive effect was even greater when the feedback was delayed. It is possible that this is because it takes advantage of the spacing effect - a gap in time between study and restudy or retrieval - and that the feedback provides a second chance for the information to be brought out of the long-term memory and considered. Researcher Robert Bjork lists this effect as an example of a *desirable difficulty*.[8] This is something that may impede performance in the short term (pupils are more likely to do well initially if they study everything in a block without any gap at all), but will lead to benefits in the long term as what pupils learn will be more secure: they will be able to access it for longer.

I occasionally hear concerns that retrieval practice is simply encouraging the learning of individual facts by rote and that although it may help you to remember that specific piece of information, it doesn't help you do anything with it. Research by Elizabeth Bjork et al., however, suggests that not only do pupils remember the facts they are quizzed on, but they actually do better on questions that are only related to these facts, which they weren't directly quizzed on.[9] Retrieval really does promote *meaningful* learning.

However it works, asking pupils to retrieve things they learnt previously is an effective way to start a lesson and helps to explain why recap plays an important role in the classroom.

7 Andrew C. Butler and Henry L. Roediger, III, Feedback enhances the positive effects and reduces the negative effects of multiple-choice testing, *Memory and Cognition* 36(3) (2008): 604–616.

8 Robert A. Bjork, Memory and metamemory considerations in the training of human beings. In Janet Metcalfe and Arthur P. Shimamura (eds), *Metacognition: Knowing About Knowing* (Cambridge, MA: MIT Press, 1994), pp. 185–215.

9 Elizabeth Ligon Bjork, Jeri L. Little and Benjamin C. Storm, Multiple-choice testing as a desirable difficulty in the classroom, *Journal of Applied Research in Memory and Cognition* 3(3) (2014): 165–170.

DEVELOPING SCHEMAS

The second reason to build recap into your lessons is to help pupils develop schemas in your subject. David Didau and Nick Rose say that "a schema can be thought of as an organising framework representing some aspect of the world and a system of organising that information".[10] A schema could be thought of as a web that connects different pieces of information together and allows this information to be brought to mind and used.

For example, an English teacher will probably have a well-developed schema around the character of Lady Macbeth. Just seeing the character's name will bring up a range of associations: the play she is in, her relationship to the other characters, key quotes and key scenes. It will also be attached to a lot of secondary information: the portrayal of women in literature, similarities and differences to how other characters are presented in Shakespeare, and performances of this character in the theatre.

Ask this teacher, "Was Lady Macbeth mad at the beginning of the play?" and their schema will come into operation. Even if they haven't considered this question before, they will be able to use what they know to provide a thoughtful answer without recourse to the text or to additional research. Their working memory will not need to hold a lot of additional information, as what they need will already be available in their long-term memory. This matters because the amount of new information we can hold in our working memory is very limited, but the amount we can store in our long-term memory is, to all extents and purposes, limitless.[11]

It is this ability to draw on an existing schema that separates an expert in a subject from a novice.[12] If a novice were to try to answer the same question, they would need to go back to the text, pick out relevant information and hold this in their working memory, then research portrayals of madness in Elizabethan theatre - and hold onto this - and then consider the form their answer should take. This is likely to overload their working memory and lead to them being unable to complete the

10 David Didau and Nick Rose, *What Every Teacher Needs to Know About Psychology* (Woodbridge: John Catt Educational, 2016), p. 19.

11 Nelson Cowan, The magical mystery four: how is working memory capacity limited, and why?, *Current Directions in Psychological Science* 19(1) (2010): 51-57.

12 John Sweller, Cognitive load during problem solving: effects on learning, *Cognitive Science* 12(2) (1988): 257-285 at 259.

task without scaffolding and support (see Chapter 3). Without this, they will fall back on more familiar knowledge and use this to answer the question. Consequently, their answer will lack depth and sophistication.

This helps to explain why the development of schemas is important, but what does that have to do with recapping previous learning? Recapping allows pupils to consider new information in terms of what they already know. As Daniel Willingham explains, "students come to understand new ideas by relating them to old ideas."[13] It might seem obvious to us, as experts, that their previous lessons on development should help them to understand the causes of deforestation in Brazil, or their work on the development of Manet's work should help them to understand the techniques used by the Impressionists, but if we don't make it explicit, these links will be lost to a novice.

Recapping, then, can be seen as a way of drawing previous learning out of a pupil's long-term memory so that they can link it to what they are about to learn. "Last lesson we looked at the level of development in Brazil" becomes "Last lesson we looked at the level of development in Brazil; you can now understand why deforestation has taken place." The more explicit we can make these links between lessons, the better we are able to help pupils develop secure schemas.

USING RETRIEVAL

As we have discussed, the effectiveness of asking pupils to retrieve information from their long-term memories is well established. The start of the lesson is often the perfect time to do this as you can review what they learnt previously without breaking the flow of the lesson by referring back to things that may not currently be relevant and thus reintroducing too much additional information. This unnecessary detail adds what John Sweller terms *extraneous load*.[14] This idea comes from his cognitive load theory, a model which suggests that we can, if we are not careful, overload a person's limited working memory and so create a barrier to learning. A

---

13 Daniel T. Willingham, *Why Don't Students Like School? A Cognitive Scientist Answers Questions About How the Mind Works and What It Means for the Classroom* (San Francisco, CA: Jossey-Bass, 2009), p. 103.

14 John Sweller, Jeroen J. G. van Merrienboer and Fred G. W. C. Paas, Cognitive architecture and instructional design, *Educational Psychology Review* 10(3) (1998): 251–296.

pupil can't think about everything presented to them and so they can't create long-term memories of the content.

The most common way of retrieving information at the start of a lesson is probably through questioning. "Last lesson we ..." quickly becomes "Who can remember what we looked at last lesson?" This is then followed up with further questions to drill down into the main points in the topic of study. A potential problem with this approach is one that is common to questioning more generally: you run the risk that only some pupils are actively trying to recollect the last lesson from memory, whilst the others are listening to their recap and are therefore restudying instead.[15]

A second, increasingly common, way for teachers to take advantage of retrieval practice at the start of the lesson is through the use of low-stakes quizzes. Starting the lesson with a quiz is a highly effective and efficient way to begin. Efficient because quizzes are very quick to produce and can be used with several classes – and even for several years – and effective because they mean all pupils are engaged in trying to recall the information from their long-term memories.

The simplest way to begin a lesson with a quiz is to list ten questions on a slide. These questions need to elicit short answers that are either right or wrong, and pupils can respond in the back of their exercise books. Answers can be placed on the next slide and pupils can mark their own work and get immediate feedback, enhancing the testing effect. It ensures that the quiz is low stakes (as pupils are not worried about you knowing what they got right or wrong) and it keeps your marking down.

The questions can be drawn from a previous lesson or from further back in the course, or a mixture of the two. You can also have a look in the back of pupils' books to see which questions they got wrong and revisit those again in the future. Education researcher Graham Nuthall suggests that pupils need to encounter the same information three times before they truly learn it.[16] Recap which systematically returns to previously taught topics helps to ensure that this reencountering occurs.

Although these kinds of low-stakes quizzes are a great way to start a lesson, they are not the only way to take advantage of retrieval practice.

---

15 Magdalena Abel and Henry L. Roediger, III, The testing effect in a social setting: does retrieval practice benefit a listener?, *Journal of Experimental Psychology: Applied* 24(3) (2018): 347–359.

16 Graham Nuthall, *The Hidden Lives of Learners* (Wellington: NZCER Press, 2007), p. 63.

Think back, plan forward

You might want to adapt the way in which you create quizzes. Usually teachers choose questions from previous topics that have no relation to the current lesson. This is missing a trick. Instead, pick questions from previous topics that help pupils to recall the information that they will be applying in this lesson. For example, before teaching a lesson on the impact of deforestation, I might pick questions that link to the nutrient cycle, the water cycle and development. This will help the pupils to see how this lesson connects to what they have learnt before (thereby building their schema on this topic), and it still takes advantage of retrieval practice.

Analyse this

Show pupils an image of something that relates to a previous topic. Give them some prompt questions to consider, which rely on them thinking back to what they have previously been taught. These could include questions about chronology ("When would this picture have been taken? Before or after X?") or about processes ("How many things might have shaped this landscape?"). These more open-ended questions require pupils to recall and use a wider range of their accrued knowledge and understanding.

Just a minute

This is a firm favourite of mine, which is based on the long-running BBC Radio 4 game. Place pupils in pairs and ask one of them to speak for a minute on a previously studied topic without hesitation, repetition or deviation. Their partner jumps in and takes over the topic if they make a mistake. This is also a useful opportunity for formative assessment. As pupils are engaged in this task, circulate the room and observe what they are able to recall, and listen out for any misconceptions that are being shared. These can then be addressed whilst they are still fresh in everyone's minds.

Connect four

Give pupils pictures that relate to four seemingly disparate topics and ask them to find as many links between the pictures as they can. To use my deforestation example, you could have a picture of deforestation in the Amazon, one of overcrowding in Rio de Janeiro, another of ships loaded with timber and, finally, a climate graph for the region. Again, the aim is to have them think hard about what they know about these topics to find the links. It also has the advantage of helping them to think like an expert in your subject, and to develop the complex web of links that the discipline depends upon.

RECAP THROUGHOUT

Although Barak Rosenshine talks about effective teachers using the start of the lesson to review previously learnt material, it is not the only time when these links will be made. Most subjects are highly synoptic: one topic builds on another and what we learn today is based on what we already know. As a result, we often need to refer back to previous lessons whilst we are teaching. Although this happens quite naturally at times, it is worth actively seeking out opportunities to do so.

Use of images

One way in which these revisits can be achieved is to use the same images in subsequent lessons. For example, when we are looking at Lagos, I will use different photos of the city to highlight various opportunities and challenges faced by its inhabitants. When looking at London, I can use those same images of Lagos to remind the class of the challenges that they are aware of in other cities before they explore the similarities and differences. I can use the same graph when illustrating growing demands for water in the UK as when looking at the need for water transfer schemes.

Questioning

Retrieval also comes up through questioning. You might ask pupils to reflect back on the message they took from *The Crucible* when studying *Animal Farm* or to think back to their work on photosynthesis when considering carbon fertilisation. As mentioned before, a potential issue with using questioning as a form of retrieval practice is that only the pupil you ask is attempting to recall the answer. Whilst the rest of the class wait to have it delivered from this person's long-term memory, theirs is untroubled. A solution is to get into the habit of asking the question, pausing a few seconds whilst everyone thinks, and then selecting a pupil to answer it. Everyone soon realises that it might be them who is called on and so they had better get thinking!

Cornell notes

Another way to build in retrieval throughout the lesson is to use what is called the Cornell note system. This simple approach just involves pupils setting out their exercise book slightly differently at the start of the lesson. They need a slightly larger left-hand margin than normal and a box at the bottom of the page. They complete their classwork in the main space as normal.[17]

The magic happens at the end of the lesson. In those last few minutes (the time you would spend doing a plenary if you were teaching like somebody was watching – see Chapter 4) pupils write a few quiz questions based on their work in the left-hand column and a summary of what they have learnt in the box at the bottom of the page. They can use these questions to quiz themselves when they come to revise. And all without you having to lift a finger.

17 For an example see Shaun Allison, Supporting retrieval practice with Cornell note taking, *Class Teaching* [blog] (24 September 2018). Available at: https://classteaching.wordpress.com/2018/09/24/supporting-retrieval-practice-with-cornell-note-taking/.

RETRIEVAL AT HOME

When teaching like somebody was watching, I would feel under pressure to set a wide variety of homework tasks. There was even a time when we were told that we should set homework that gave pupils a choice of activities that they could select from based on their learning styles. At other times we were expected to set long projects which meant that pupils could learn "independently"[18] whilst making volcano models or composing a rap about eruptions (I really wish I were making this up). Homework was expected to be creative (without teaching pupils the skills to be creative *with*) and engaging (without a thought to what they should be engaged in). There is certainly a place for teachers to help with learning *outside* the classroom, so that a learner's understanding is taken beyond what happens *in* the classroom (see Chapter 6), but I would suggest it isn't here.

Some schools also like to use a homework timetable to govern when staff should set homework in each subject. The intention here is often good - to ensure that pupils aren't overloaded with homework on any given day - but all too often they are really used as a way of ensuring that teachers are setting homework. This leads to the ridiculous situation in which teachers quickly set something just because they have to, rather than because they need to. If we were to set homework like nobody was watching, we would set tasks because we feel that they have a real benefit for our pupils, without leading to an increase in workload for us. They would be simple tasks that maximise learning in the minimum amount of time, and they would use retrieval. As a result, I am now much more likely to set homework which involves pupils doing retrieval practice. It might not be glamorous, but it works. Revision, to be effective, needs to be an ongoing process. So the kinds of activities you might do closer to exams really need to become part of their regular homework.

Rather than setting homework tasks based on the work pupils are currently doing, set homework on topics they covered previously. Try to make these tasks things that they can complete from memory (taking advantage of the testing effect), rather than expecting them to use notes or study guides. This might include producing concept maps of previous topics, answering short quiz questions or longer exam-style questions, drawing diagrams or summarising chapters. The key is that the task is done from memory. This is a very efficient way of using homework to make sure

18 See Chapter 2 for reasons why this was probably a bad idea.

that revision becomes the responsibility of the pupils, and it can remove the need for you to run revision sessions. It becomes even more efficient as they should be able to check their own work - as, in many cases, they will have the answers in their notes.

The Cornell note system is even more efficient as you don't even need to set the questions: the pupils have done that themselves. You can simply ask them to answer their own review questions on a given topic and then give them a short quiz on it at the start of the next lesson.

DEVELOPING SCHEMAS

Many of the techniques used for retrieval practice that we've explored so far will also help pupils to develop schemas about the topic (making them not only effective but efficient too!). However, there are things that we can do specifically with the aim of encouraging pupils to make mental links between their lessons. As with retrieval practice, it is a mistake to see this as something that only happens at the start of the lesson during some kind of starter. Instead, we need to see it as an integral part of the teaching process.

Hook it

The term "hook", as used in education, has evolved in meaning over the years. When I started teaching - when I taught like *everybody* was watching - we were encouraged to use something to hook pupils' interest, to engage them in the learning process. I remember being told that I should use icebreaker activities at the start of a lesson to get a class up, moving around and talking so that they would be hooked into the learning. They would do things like finding someone else in the room with the same type of pet as them, or someone who liked the same flavour ice cream. The hook, such as it was, was utterly divorced from what was being learnt and the idea, I believe, was simply to lull them into a false sense of security so that they didn't see the learning sneaking up on them. It felt as though there was a dominant belief that education was being imposed on children, and so we needed to do all we could to mitigate against this through planning fun little activities and distractions.

Now when we talk about "hooks" it is in the context of pupils connecting what they are about to learn with what they already know. The days of tricking kids into learning are behind us and we can instead just let our subjects shine. As discussed, Willingham shows us how pupils understand new ideas in relation to what they already know. It is therefore important to create a hook for new information so that it is anchored to their existing schemas. If this doesn't happen, then not only is any new information going to be pretty useless - how will it be applied if it doesn't connect to anything else? - but it is going to be difficult to retrieve as well, as little will prompt the recall of it.[19] For example, if you knew nothing about rivers and I told you that helicoidal flow is a contributing factor in the creation of slip-off slopes and river cliffs on a meander, it is unlikely that you would remember this tomorrow or be able to make use of the information.

Instead, I would need to link this information to something you already know, to a part of your schema attached to rivers. I could ask you to picture a local river you have visited or show you an image of a river. I could remind you of the lessons we have done on rivers and how water acts in a meander and add a reminder of what happens when you are in a car that drives around a corner too fast. I could also remind you of the root of the word "helicoidal", meaning "to spin". A reminder of what you already know about rivers has created a hook for this new information and so allowed it to be attached to the existing schema.

We can create these hooks by making the links between topics explicit. One way to achieve this is to show the connections between lessons by calling up the resources used in previous lessons or having pupils review their work from relevant previous lessons (this is especially easy to do if you are using the Cornell note system). These kinds of activities can replace some of those flashy "engaging" starter tasks that we were once encouraged to deploy. Instead of spending hours trying to create some sort of event in the first five minutes of the lesson, we can let pupils know that when they come into the classroom, they will be directed to look back at their notes from a particular lesson and complete some review questions. They are then good to go.

19 For more on this see the theory of disuse from Elizabeth Ligon Bjork and Robert A. Bjork, Intentional forgetting can increase, not decrease, residual influences of to-be-forgotten information, *Journal of Experimental Psychology: Learning, Memory, and Cognition* 29(4) (2003): 524-531.

Thread it through

Of course, we don't only see teachers recapping at the start of lessons. Excellent teachers are forever referring back to previous learning. They know that this will slow the pace of the lesson but that it will make that learning all the more meaningful. We can thread the development of schemas through a lesson by deliberately interweaving relevant previous topics into the current one (see Chapter 5). We can create tasks that require pupils to use what they have studied in the past in the present. For example, you might:

- Ask pupils to reflect on the feudal system, which they studied at the start of the year, when considering the impact of the Black Death.
- Expect pupils to include their knowledge of relief rainfall patterns when evaluating the proposed site of a new reservoir.
- Require pupils to draw on the presentation of communism in *Animal Farm* when answering questions on *The Crucible*.

This will hopefully lead to pupils considering what they have learnt in the light of new information and making meaningful connections between topics, of the sort that experts deploy.

We can also thread the development of schemas through the learning by flagging up what pupils still don't know and linking it to topics to come, thus preparing the way for new information. We can end a lesson by asking, "What more do we need to know to make sense of this?" As such, we look both ways and think about when we might recap this current lesson in the future.

Reveal the picture

The development of schemas is all about creating a big picture of our subject from the threads of individual lessons or snippets of information. We are completing a jigsaw puzzle and it helps to show pupils what they are working towards: they need to see the front of the box.

One way to do this is to create knowledge organisers for each topic, which incorporate an outline of the big picture. Knowledge organisers are summary sheets that highlight the key knowledge that a pupil is expected to remember and, as such, they are an intrinsically useful way to help make a schema explicit. They can go further, though, by including details on how this topic links to previous studies or to things that will come later.

We can also make the big picture explicit in a much more literal sense by including a display in our classrooms or in departmental corridors. These displays can show the topics that pupils will study and the links between them. In geography, for example, we might place the study of Haiti in the centre of the board and then show how the topics relating to plate tectonics, weather hazards, development studies and international trade will all be used in this unit.

For us to make the big picture explicit to pupils we need to have a very clear image of it ourselves. It is important that we see the links between topics and lessons, and are able to identify natural opportunities for interweaving. This is why considerations about the curriculum will play such a big role in Part II.

AVOIDING RECAP PITFALLS

Recapping previous learning is such a natural part of teaching that there should be very few pitfalls. Unfortunately, the overcomplications that are a constant enemy of those teaching like nobody's watching are insidious and can be found even here. These are a few potential difficulties to watch out for.

There is a pressure in teaching to show that lessons have "good pace". No one seems to be able to define exactly what this means, but feedback from lesson observations seems to imply it means "getting through things quickly". Recap, by its very nature, involves slowing things down and taking some time to look back at what has come before, instead of hurtling towards the future. Sometimes it can feel like there isn't time to build recap into a lesson as there is too much content to cover. However, this is part of a "culture of doing" that puts covering material ahead of learning it. We need to be willing to slow down.

Pupils will often prefer restudy to retrieval. Remembering things that we have looked at in the past is difficult; this is exactly why we are practising it. If recall were easy, we wouldn't need to spend time on it. This difficulty can lead to pupils wanting to use notes to help them remember, and teachers capitulating. It is hard to leave a pupil struggling, especially if we are worried about an outside observer wondering why we aren't stepping in to help them. However, the aim of retrieval practice is to exert the effort of recall. If we look back at our notes, we are restudying - and not recalling - and we won't be taking advantage of the testing effect. We can overcome this by teaching pupils *why* these methods will be less effective.

Humans have an insatiable desire for novelty. Studies show that people will eat more sweets if they are in a range of colours than if they are all of the same appearance.[20] We seek out difference. This can lead to teachers worrying that if they start every lesson with a recap of previous learning, as suggested by Barak Rosenshine, pupils will be bored and disengaged. It is worth remembering, however, that, firstly, pupils are only in your lessons for a couple of hours a week. They get plenty of novelty in their day. Secondly, there are many ways of recapping previous learning, as we have discussed. There is no reason why the start of the lesson always has to be the same, but nor is there a reason why it shouldn't be.

KEY POINTS

- Recapping previously learnt material is a natural part of the learning process.
- We recap both to take advantage of the testing effect and to help develop our learners' schemas.
- The testing effect states that retrieving knowledge from our long-term memory makes it easier to recall in the future.
- This testing effect can be achieved not only through testing but through any activity that requires pupils to recall what they have previously learnt.
- Schemas are the web of knowledge we have about a topic. The schema of an expert is more developed than that of a novice.
- When we teach like nobody's watching, we can use the start of a lesson for recap rather than engagement.

---

20 Barbara E. Kahn and Brian Wansink, The influence of assortment structure on perceived variety and consumption quantities, *Journal of Consumer Research* 30(4) (2004): 519-533.

REFLECTIONS

- Think back to your last lesson. How much of it was based on something pupils had learnt in the past?
- How can you connect pupils' previous learning to what you are about to teach them?
- Create a mind map on the knowledge used in your next lesson. How many connections can you find to other topics in two minutes?
- Think about your next lesson. What recap questions could you ask to check what pupils have learnt and allow them to practise recall?

CHAPTER 2

INPUT

FROM THE CHALKFACE

I started teaching in the early noughties. Looking back now, a lot of the advice (more non-negotiable instruction really) we received seems bizarre, but at the time it was all we knew. Perhaps the strangest instruction was for the teacher to say as little as possible in class and to avoid telling pupils things. This would be "teaching" and we were there to "facilitate their learning". What this led to was asking pupils to discuss questions they didn't know how to answer in the hope that they would somehow stumble upon key insights. I remember being praised after one lesson observation as I hadn't spoken to the whole class at all. The fact that their work was terrible didn't seem to matter to the observer. I hadn't ruined the lesson by teaching them anything, and thus robbing them of the chance of discovery.

These days I tend to tell them things.

THE IMPORTANCE OF INPUT

Input matters. In their report for The Sutton Trust, Robert Coe and his team found that quality of instruction was one of the most significant factors in determining the success of a lesson.[1] This makes sense, as what we learn has to come from somewhere. Whilst we can learn all kinds of things from experience in our day-to-day lives, schools are there to provide an education in those things that we can't just intuit.

In *Seven Myths About Education*, Daisy Christodoulou makes the point that there is a difference between things that humans learn simply from exposure – like language and social skills – and those things we only learn because we are deliberately taught them – like reading or using a number system.[2] And yet this seemingly obvious point has, as she shows in that book, been highly controversial.

When I started teaching, we were encouraged to limit the amount of input we gave in a lesson. There was a feeling that it was somehow cheating to give pupils the answers and, as I was told during one memorable CPD session, "rob them of the chance of discovery". This idea has deep roots in the writing of Jean-Jacques Rousseau, John Dewey and Paulo Freire, who each, in their way, rejected a transmission model of education (between an expert who has knowledge and a novice who doesn't) in favour of a constructionist model whereby the pupil creates new knowledge through having authentic experiences.[3]

As a result of these ideas we were told things like "if you are talking, they aren't learning", that listening was "passive" and as such didn't lead to learning, and that we should be "a guide on the side, not a sage on the stage". It even got to the point where teachers were timed by observers to ensure they didn't talk for more than a certain number of minutes per lesson.

---

1 Robert Coe, Cesare Aloisi, Steve Higgins and Lee Elliot Major, *What Makes Great Teaching? Review of the Underpinning Research* (London: Sutton Trust, 2014). Available at: https://www.suttontrust.com/wp-content/uploads/2014/10/What-makes-great-teaching-FINAL-4.11.14-1.pdf.

2 Christodoulou, *Seven Myths About Education*, p. 36.

3 For a fascinating discussion on the influences of progressive thinking in education see Kieran Egan, *Getting It Wrong from the Beginning: Our Progressivist Inheritance from Herbert Spencer, John Dewey, and Jean Piaget* (New Haven and London: Yale University Press, 2002).

And yet if you watch people teach naturally, you hear them speak. A lot. If someone asks you how to change a car tyre, you tell them. You talk them through it, step by step. You might draw them a diagram, make some notes and, if you are feeling kind, lend a hand, but whatever you do, you talk. If someone wanted to learn to drive a car, you'd teach them by imparting what you know and heavily guiding their practice, not just by handing over the keys.

You see the same thing in the classroom when teachers teach like nobody's watching. They talk more, and they do so because it works. Barak Rosenshine found that effective teachers spoke for an average of 23 minutes across a 40-minute lesson, whereas the least effective teachers spoke for just 11 minutes.[4] Talking more was more effective than talking less. There are similar findings from Guido Schwerdt and Amelie Wuppermann, who looked at claims that lecture-style teaching was harmful to pupil progress and found that no such thing was true.[5]

Paul Kirschner, John Sweller and Richard Clark go even further and argue that minimally guided instruction is an ineffective way for pupils to learn and that pupils learn better from the much-maligned transmission model of education.[6] One problem we now face is that teachers have endured decades of being told that they should talk less, that they should have less input into their lessons. Any problem with teacher-talk has been explained away as a fundamental flaw in the method, rather than in the individual practice. As such, despite it being a central part of any lesson, very little training is given in how to explain better. This chapter attempts to get to the heart of what makes an explanation memorable.

4 Rosenshine, Principles of instruction, 14.

5 Guido Schwerdt and Amelie C. Wuppermann, Is Traditional Teaching Really All That Bad? A Within-Student Between-Subject Approach (April 2009). CESifo Working Paper Series No. 2634. Available at: https://ssrn.com/abstract=1396620.

6 Paul A. Kirschner, John Sweller and Richard E. Clark, Why minimal guidance during instruction does not work: an analysis of the failure of constructivist, discovery, project-based, experiential, and inquiry-based teaching, *Educational Psychologist* 41(2) (2006): 75–86.

INPUT AND BEHAVIOUR MANAGEMENT

One difficult issue that needs to be addressed before we can look at effective input is that of behaviour management. It is all but impossible to teach a class - to stand at the front of the room and carefully and clearly break down and explain a complex idea - unless everyone is focused on what you are saying. Activities that are often labelled as "low level disruption" - such as talking over the teacher, flicking paper at each other or turning around to steal someone's pencil case - may look trivial in isolation, but they will mean that any attempt to deliver a lesson is futile.

When I started teaching, the idea of standing in front of the class and trying to explain something seemed like a fool's game. I knew that they wouldn't listen, that they would mess around and that any attempt to admonish them would be met with incredulity. Instead, I quickly retreated and fell back on setting independent work that they would get on with whilst I ran around the room trying to explain it to each group of pupils and to keep everyone on track. The behaviour was no better, and the learning a lot slower, but it was easier to ignore.

One problem I faced in those early days of my career was that we were told, repeatedly, that poor pupil behaviour was a sign of a badly planned lesson. We were also told that a noisy classroom was a sign that learning was happening and that a silent classroom, in which pupils were listening to their teacher for an extended period of time, was both unrealistic and a sign of inadequate teaching. This made it very difficult to sanction pupils for disruptive behaviour and to ask for help. Talking to many teachers over the years, it would seem that I was not alone in encountering this approach.

It is very hard to know just how far the teaching profession has moved on as discussions about behaviour are still somewhat taboo. No school wants to admit that poor behaviour is an issue and it is something that is often carefully hidden from outside observers. Anecdotally, I can say that when I go into schools and talk to teachers about teaching, one barrier to effective and efficient explanation that they often identify is that they don't believe the pupils will sit and listen to them and they are worried about being exposed at the front of the class. Likewise, when they come to observe teachers in my department, they often comment that they are amazed that pupils will sit and listen so attentively.

The reasons why our pupils will sit and listen to an extended teacher explanation are many and complex. Most will do it because we consistently make sure our explanations are well-structured, and because they are intrigued by the question we want them to answer. Most of our pupils love the enthusiasm we have for our subject and respond well to the positive relationships we always seek to build. However, as in every school there will always be a few pupils for whom none of these strategies work. No matter how clear the explanation, how intriguing the lesson and how warm and welcoming the teacher tries to be, they arrive in the classroom determined to disrupt.

For these pupils, the things that have made the difference are very clear routines and expectations. We sweat the small stuff so that they don't have to. Here are a few questions to think about:

- How should pupils come into your room?
- Should pupils write down the title and the date as soon as they come in?
- Is there always a task that they should do when they arrive?
- Are they allowed to sit slumped in their chair with their head on the desk whilst you are talking?
- Should they be holding their pens whilst you talk?
- Can they doodle in the margins of their books whilst you are talking?

By being very clear on these seemingly minor points we make the lives of our pupils much easier. If we are not consistent - for example, they can sometimes get away with running into the room shouting to their friends, but they sometimes get a sanction; one day they can rest their head on the desk and the next they get in trouble; one day you want them to start working as soon as they come in and the next you want them to wait - you are just creating opportunities for conflict and confusion. They now need to spend time thinking about what it is you want, rather than about the content of the lesson.

If this still doesn't work, then we need to use the school's behaviour policy and use it consistently (see Part III). If we are unable to teach, then we are unable to teach like nobody's watching!

INPUT IN THE CLASSROOM

Subject knowledge

The same Sutton Trust report that highlights the quality of instruction as being pivotal in a lesson also affords status to a teacher's knowledge about their subject. The link between the two should be clear: it is impossible to provide high-quality instruction about something you know nothing about. The first step in ensuring that you can give effective input in the classroom is to know your subject very well.

When we know a topic well, we can explain it with a great deal more clarity and confidence. We have the topic well embedded in our own schemas and so can relate it to further topics and examples to highlight key points. For example, when I am teaching about the role of appropriate technology in development, I can draw on examples of tractors rusting in north Africa or South Africa's Playpump scheme. I can link the ideas of appropriate technology and sustainability whilst also drawing my pupils' attention to the key differences between them. If, on the other hand, my knowledge of this topic were limited to a simple definition of the term and a limited understanding of its criteria, I wouldn't be able to add this level of richness and thus develop my pupils' schemas by revealing my own.

Indeed, you may notice this yourself when reading the example I've just given. You may have north Africa in your schema, but is there anything connecting it to agricultural technology? You may be able to hazard a guess as to what a "playpump" does, but does your schema reveal how it links to the appropriateness of different technologies in South Africa? Does your schema link to enough additional information about the development needs of rural South Africa for you to do this? If your subject knowledge is lacking, you can't deliver a successful input.

There are many ways in which we can continue to develop our subject knowledge throughout our careers. The simplest, and perhaps most rewarding, is to just continue immersing yourself in the literature of your subject. It can, of course, be difficult to make time to sit and read a book or an article when it feels like there is so much else that needs doing. This is symptomatic of the way in which teachers' professional knowledge has been sidelined as workload has increased. The only solution is to recognise the importance of maintaining your subject knowledge and therefore schedule time to do so - the same way you would plan in time to mark a pile of tests. Hopefully the advice in this book will help you to streamline your teaching by making it more efficient, and thus help you find the time to do this.

A potential difficulty of relying on professional books and journals to maintain your knowledge is the time lag between a development in your subject and these developments reaching your classroom. It can take a long time for the ideas of academia to filter down into the books we might pick up and read in our local bookshop. A second issue is that the content can feel very far removed from the subject at a school level. The information needs to be recontextualised from an academic setting into a school one.[7] This is one area in which subject associations can play an important part. Most have regular journals, featuring articles on both teaching the subject and improving the teacher's subject knowledge. For example, The Geographical Association have recently published articles on the changing ideas about tectonic movement, and the implications for the classroom, and a strand looking at knowledge of the new Changing Spaces, Making Places A level unit.[8]

Subject associations also offer training sessions and conferences where new ideas can be shared and discussed, and knowledge built. As well as the conferences run by official subject associations there are also an increasing number of subject-specific TeachMeet events being organised by teachers around the UK. These events, which are almost always free to attend, tend to be held in the evening or at weekends, and feature contributions from a number of attendees.

The rise of social media has certainly made developing subject knowledge easier than ever before, with communities of teachers willing to not only share resources but also discuss aspects of subject knowledge and share articles and books of interest.

Scripting and practice

Once we accept that a teacher's input is a vital part of the lesson, we may need to change the focus for our lesson preparation and planning: the attention switches

7 See, for example, Roger Firth, Recontextualising geography as a school subject. In Mark Jones and David Lambert (eds), *Debates in Geography Education*, 2nd edn (Abingdon: Routledge, 2018), pp. 275–286.

8 See https://www.geography.org.uk/Journals/Teaching-Geography.

from spending long periods of time trying to plan exciting activities[9] to spending more time planning memorable explanation.

In *Mining for Gold*, Fergal Roche recounts stories of effective teachers who he has encountered over his life. Some taught him, others are individuals he worked with or led. One attribute that recurs throughout the book is the level of preparation that these teachers put into their explanation. He says of one teacher, Peter Hardwick, "He must have spent hours preparing. He had endless bits of paper in front of him on which he had scrawled his notes about the literature we were studying."[10] In 15 years of teaching, and in the countless lessons I have observed, I can't think of a single occasion in which I have seen a teacher refer to their notes when giving an explanation. It could be argued that this is because the teacher's knowledge about a topic – their schema – is so developed that these notes are unnecessary. However, I would argue that there are reasons why using notes might make our teaching more effective and efficient.

- **Structure.** Whilst we may have the knowledge of what we want to explain, the way in which we structure this explanation is vitally important. If a history teacher wants to explain the impact of the Black Death on the changes to the feudal system, they need to consider how to introduce each element so that pupils can best make sense of it. It means we can avoid explanations that ramble on, with new information added sporadically as the speaker remembers to include it.
- **Concise.** As we have seen, and will go on to discuss further momentarily, there is a limit to a person's working memory. We don't want to overload them with unnecessary information. Having our explanation roughly planned out can help us to avoid tangents that might occur in the moment but could lead to simply confusing the class.
- **Depth.** Our own working memory is limited. Whilst, as subject experts, we will have committed a lot of information to our long-term memory and will be able to retrieve it, there might still be occasions when we want to draw on a wealth of specific facts and figures to support our explanation.

9 For a discussion on the problems with exciting activities see Chapter 3.
10 Fergal Roche, *Mining for Gold: Stories of Effective Teachers* (Woodbridge: John Catt Educational, 2017), p. 18.

- **Supports.** When we plan an explanation, we don't only include those things we want to say, but the things we will use to support what we say. It gives us the space to consider the analogies we might use ("Air moves from areas of high pressure to areas of low pressure - think about what happens if you let the air out of a balloon you are inflating.") or the diagrams we want to draw to help show a process (we'll explore this further when we look at dual coding).
- **Efficiency.** Of course, much of this book is about how to make our teaching more efficient, to save ourselves time and energy. It might therefore seem counterintuitive for me to be suggesting that we add to our workload. However, planning our explanation can save us a huge amount of time in the long run:
  - Firstly, it reduces the need to give feedback. If our explanation is unclear then pupils develop misconceptions, which appear in their work and then need correcting. If our explanation is clear, pupils make fewer mistakes and our marking load reduces enormously.
  - Secondly, we can reuse our notes for years to come. I know I will always need to explain the atmospheric circulation model. It seems highly unlikely that much is going to change in our understanding of how this operates, so spending ten minutes planning out an excellent way to explain it now is going to save me hours of angst in years to come.
  - Thirdly, we can use these notes to help us collaborate. If our notes are detailed enough, they can be shared with others in the department or across schools. There is an odd stigma around using someone else's explanation in your class - and using a script to teach from - as though it is unprofessional. Oddly, we seem to be much happier to take an activity developed by another teacher or to use a video clip of someone else explaining something. If one teacher has an excellent way of explaining covalent bonds, rich in analogies and examples, why shouldn't another teacher use it to support their own delivery? (For more on collaborative planning see Chapter 8.)

This final point on sharing scripts brings us to the programme of direct instruction developed by Siegfried Engelmann and colleagues in the 1960s. In this programme, teachers were provided with very explicit instructions on what to teach and how. The goal was to maximise how much was learnt by children in each lesson, with the aim of closing the gap between the more disadvantaged children and those who came from wealthier homes. As part of the programme, teachers were given scripts. The rationale being that "the scripts provide teachers with directions, sequences of examples, and sequences of subskills and wordings that already have been tested for effectiveness."[11]

This method was investigated by Project Follow Through, which contrasted the progress made by pupils following a wide range of different teaching methods, and was found to be the most effective.[12] Despite this proven effectiveness and efficiency, scripted lessons have never really caught on or been more widely accepted by the profession or by those who lead and train us. However, they arguably have a place in the arsenal of any teacher who is teaching like nobody's watching.

Working memory

One reason why teacher input has had such an image problem is the prevalent use of Edgar Dale's Cone of Learning in teacher training and CPD. Even if you don't recognise the name you would almost certainly recognise it if you saw it: it is a pyramid purporting to show how much a child recalls following different types of activities. At the top of the pyramid - i.e. the least effective - we have things like listening to a teacher and reading at 10%, and at the bottom "learning from doing" at 90%.

This image should set off warning bells immediately. Firstly, no research gives us such lovely round numbers that fit together so neatly in a pyramid. Secondly, it can't possibly be true that we remember 10% of *anything* we read: some things must be more memorable than others. Thirdly, we each have our own experiences and interests, and this must surely shape what we absorb. I can remember large parts of interesting talks I have heard on topics I have an interest in but certainly can't remember 90% of what I did last month. In fact, Dale's Cone of Learning originally

11 Siegfried Engelmann, Wesley C. Becker, Douglas Carnine and Russell Gersten, The direct instruction follow through model: design and outcomes, *Education and Treatment of Children* 11(4) (1988): 303–317 at 306.

12 See https://www.nifdi.org/what-is-di/project-follow-through.

had nothing to do with learning and contained no nice round numbers; instead, it was a theoretical model to show how authentic an experience was.[13]

However, like many examples of faddish thinking, the idea of limiting teacher-talk because it is forgettable does contain a kernel of truth. Teacher explanation won't lead to learning if it overloads a pupil's working memory. The problem with verbal instruction is that the words are fleeting and there is a limit to how much new information we can hold in our heads. The answer isn't to speak less, but to plan our explanations to support pupils' working memories and help it to stick. We can do this in a number of ways:

- **Keep it relevant.** John Sweller talks about different types of cognitive load, of which we have already encountered extraneous.[14] Intrinsic load is something we can do little about as it is linked to the complexity of the task that we want pupils to do (i.e. it is either a difficult thing to comprehend or it isn't - one example could be the difference between solving a simple sum and solving simultaneous equations). Germane load (a term that John Sweller now rarely uses) refers to the ability to build complex schemas and transfer information into new contexts. Extraneous load, as we have seen, is created by the way in which information is presented. Some facts are useful to the task at hand and others are nothing but undesirable distractions. We want to make sure that what we say is relevant and useful, and that we avoid drifting off on tangents, however interesting they may seem at the time. All these little tangents just add more information that our pupils are then trying to keep in their heads until they can decide what is relevant and what isn't. This increases the cognitive load of the task.
- **Break it up.** As we have seen, Barak Rosenshine found that the most effective teachers spoke for more minutes in a lesson, but they didn't speak in one block. They explained, then pupils applied the explanation to a task, then there was more explanation and then more practice. In this way, pupils have the chance to do something with the new information in their working memory,

13 For a detailed look at the history, and continued influence, of the Cone of Learning, see Will Thalheimer, Mythical retention data and the corrupted cone, *Work-Learning Research* [blog] (5 January 2015). Available at https://www.worklearning.com/2015/01/05/mythical-retention-data-the-corrupted-cone/.

14 John Sweller, Element interactivity and intrinsic, extraneous, and germane cognitive load, *Educational Psychology Review* 22(2) (2010): 123–138.

improving the likelihood of embedding it in their long-term memory and thus increasing its durability.

- **Avoid distractions.** If you have ever sat adding up the marks on an exam paper, you will know how important it is to avoid distractions. If someone comes along and interrupts your calculation, you have to start again. The same is true for our pupils. If they are following your explanation of the significance of the word "nothing" in *Hamlet* and someone comes to the door with a message, their train of thought has been disrupted. This is one reason why learning only really happens when behaviour is impeccable. If you are disrupted, you need to start the explanation from the beginning.
- **Leave a trace.** Words are ephemeral. Once they are said they linger in the working memory and then are gone. We can support working memory by offloading some of the information onto another source. Write key points on the board during an explanation or record them as a flow diagram, showing your thought process. It could be that not everyone needs these notes as support. Leave a mini whiteboard on particular pupils' desks and add prompts as and when they need them. Alternatively, teach pupils how to make their own notes during your explanation so that they can refer back to them later.

A great deal of effective teaching, especially when it comes to instruction, is about managing the limitations of working memory. We need to keep in mind that there is a limit to how much new information a person can keep in their head at any one time. That doesn't mean we should limit teacher-talk, it just means we should learn to do it better.

Dual coding

One way in which we can support working memory is by taking advantage of the principles of dual coding, developed in the 1970s by Allan Paivio.[15] This theory suggests that people take in information through two channels: visual and auditory. Our auditory channel is used for what we hear but also for what we read, whereas our visual channel takes in everything we see.

15 For a discussion on the development of dual coding see Allan Paivio, Dual coding theory: retrospect and current status, *Canadian Journal of Psychology* 45(3) (1991): 255-287.

This theory holds some important implications for how we teach. Firstly, we need to ensure that we don't overload one of these channels. The most common way in which this happens is when we ask pupils to read a text whilst hearing it read out loud. This makes it more difficult to follow. Think about the difficulty you might face if trying to watch a film which is subtitled in your own language. Your attention is constantly split between these two sources of information. Despite this problem, it is something that teachers are frequently encouraged to do - the idea of pupils just listening to something being read to them seeming too "passive" once again.

Secondly, we can use these insights to support our explanation by including diagrams and images to accompany our narration. Research by Richard Mayer and Richard Anderson found that when verbal explanation was accompanied by diagrams it was significantly more memorable than when presented as either form on its own.[16] This is why you'll see experienced teachers instinctively heading to the whiteboard to draw diagrams to help explain difficult concepts.

For this to be effective it is important that the images and diagrams we use are relevant to the spoken explanation and are carefully chosen to support it. Crowding a PowerPoint slide or worksheet with images simply to make it more attractive is going to add extraneous load to pupils' working memories and make it harder for them to focus on what is important to the explanation or task.

Storytelling

Daniel Willingham suggests that humans are predisposed to remember information that is presented as a story.[17] There is something about the rhythm and structure of a story that makes it stick in our minds. Stories are interesting, easy to understand and easy to remember. He shows that this is the case because human minds seek causal relationships (this happened because this happened, which led to this happening), and it is these kinds of relationships on which stories are built.

---

16 Richard E. Mayer and Richard B. Anderson, Animations need narrations: an experimental test of a dual-coding hypothesis, *Journal of Educational Psychology* 83(4) (1991): 484–490.

17 Daniel T. Willingham, Ask the cognitive scientist: the privileged status of story, *American Educator* (summer 2004). Available at: https://www.aft.org/periodical/american-educator/summer-2004/ask-cognitive-scientist.

We can exploit the inherent stickability of stories by framing our explanations in this way. Many subjects involve the exploration of causal relationships: in geography we have the story of how erosion led to the formation of chalk stacks in Dorset, in history there is the story of the causes of the First World War and in science we have the story of how humans evolved.

To take the first example, we can start by flagging up that a story is about to begin: "I want to tell you how Old Harry got left alone in the sea." Then we can create the character of Old Harry using the features we want our pupils to recall: the hard, white chalk and the added complication that he is weakened with fractures. Now we have conflict: it is Old Harry against the sea, holding out for as long as he can but doomed to fail. All the way through we have causality - this is happening because the thing before happened.

This story gives us the four Cs that, according to Willingham, make a story stick:

1 Causality
2 Conflict
3 Complications
4 Character

In the case of the science lesson on human evolution, we have the character of humanity, the conflict with the environment, the complications of this environment changing and the causality of biological adaptation to these changes.

Closely linked to the idea of storytelling is the use of analogies and examples, which help bring an explanation to life. The intent behind using an analogy is to make the abstract and distant seem familiar and closer. You are showing the pupils that this thing they are unfamiliar with can be understood by relating it to something they recognise. For example, pupils may have difficulty picturing how the expansion of water as it freezes cracks rock, but they have experienced what happens to a bottle of water when they put it in the freezer overnight. They may struggle with the idea of hot air rising, but can picture it in the form of the hot-air balloon from the film *Up*.

When planning the use of analogies in teaching, working in collaboration really helps. Teachers tend to develop a bank of analogies over the years and these can easily be shared and adopted by others. It is important, though, to consider the context of the analogy. They only work if they are familiar to the person hearing them. Using redundant technology, or an experience your pupils have never had, as an analogy is only going to add to their cognitive load, as they will struggle, firstly, to understand the analogy and, secondly, to relate it to another unfamiliar concept.

If you see teachers working like nobody's watching, you see natural storytellers. The best teachers hold their class enthralled as the story of their subject is brought to life in the pupils' heads through the use of carefully planned narratives. Only the complication of being told to limit how long we spend talking destroys this magic.

Pacing and performance

It could be argued that good teacher input, like any form of public speaking, is a performance art. Once we see it as such, we begin to see the need for careful preparation and the possible need for a script. It is worth considering not only what we say but also how we say it.

When teaching as though people were watching, I would find myself speaking quickly in an effort to get through any necessary teacher-talk and allow pupils to "start learning". Now, however, I am more aware of the need to slow down and speak carefully, so that everyone can follow what I am saying. We also need to be aware of our tone and ensure that we don't end up speaking in a dull monotone. We want our pupils' attention to be directed to what we say, so our voice needs to command their attention.

Another point to consider is where we stand and how we move. When I began teaching, it was fashionable to warn teachers against being "stuck at the front of the class" during our brief explanations. To do so risked being a "sage on the stage". Instead, we should try to talk from different points in the room. Now, there may occasionally be a good reason to talk from the back of the room - for example, when you need pupils to look at something at the front whilst you talk and you don't want to obstruct their view - but generally you need their attention on you as you speak, and the best way to achieve this is to be in front of them.

The same goes for pacing the room, which was also recommended practice. Movement can help to illustrate a point - perhaps the meandering of a river, or the movement of sediment up and down a beach through longshore drift - but if the movement doesn't add to your point, it is just extraneous load that will distract from what you are saying.

The idea that a teacher should be an entertainer hopefully belongs to another age, but it is true that we need to hold the attention of our class. Watch great orators at work. Look at their gestures, their use, or limit of, movement and listen to their use of pitch and pace to keep their audience with them. Learn from them.

Questioning

One criticism that is sometimes levelled at the increased use of teacher-talk is that this approach is didactic: that pupils are passive, switched off and simply being lectured at. However, good teacher input rarely resembles a lecture as it will contain a lot of questioning and discussion as a class.

Questioning is an element of classroom practice that is easily observable by an outsider. It is therefore not surprising that the use of questioning often gets picked up for comment by observers who try to note whether it is effective. What, then, does effective questioning look like?

One of the things that is often deemed a poor use of questioning is the teacher using closed questions. Some observers seem to hold the view that these questions are too limited. However, this misses the point. Questioning is used for a number of different functions and sometimes closed questions are entirely appropriate. One reason why we ask questions is to check for understanding. As mentioned previously, there is a limit to a pupil's working memory. As we are explaining something, we need to ensure that everyone in the class is still with us and is retaining all the salient points. Closed questions may be more appropriate than open ones when checking that this is the case.

For example, if I were teaching a lesson on causes of the Boscastle floods and stopped to ask a pupil an open question such as, "What caused the floods?" they could respond with an array of possible answers. If they say, "It was caused by heavy rain" what do I learn? Do they only know this cause? Have they missed all the others? I am still completely in the dark. In contrast, if I ask a closed question, such as, "Are the valley sides leading down to Boscastle steep or gentle?" or, "Where are the houses in the village built?", I can quickly check that pupils are following what I have said.

Open questions are best used for a different purpose: to deepen understanding. Through the use of clever questioning we can help pupils to explore an issue in more depth and also to make connections between different parts of the topic and so develop their schema (see Chapter 1). One way to do this is by using Socratic questions. Here is an example of an exchange using Socratic questions from *Making Every Geography Lesson Count*:

Teacher: Should London prioritise protecting its green space?

Student: Yes.

1. Classify their thinking.

Teacher: What do you know about the need for green space in London?

Student: It helps to prevent flooding as water can infiltrate into the soil. It also provides space for communities and tourists like it.

2. Probe assumptions.

Teacher: What would change your answer about prioritising green space?

Student: If there was another way to prevent flooding, or if something more dangerous than flooding would happen if not.

3. Demand evidence.

Teacher: What evidence is there that cities need this green space to prevent flooding?

Student: In Lagos, they built on open land in the city and flooding increased.

4. Alternative viewpoints.

Teacher: Would everyone agree that green space should be a priority in cities?

Student: No. If we don't build on this land then house prices will be more expensive. This might mean that people who can't afford a house would have different priorities.

5. Explore implications.

Teacher: What would be the implications of saying that London should prioritise green space?

Student: It would mean that the authorities would need to act to protect green space and ban building on it. It might mean that developers need to look for somewhere else to put homes, like brownfield sites.

6. Question the question.

Teacher: Why do you think we need to ask questions like this?

Student: We can't prioritise everything and need to consider what we think is most important.[18]

Outside observers sometimes criticise such exchanges by arguing that whilst you are engaging one pupil in this discussion the rest of the class are just listening. There are two responses to this from someone teaching like nobody's watching. Firstly, so what? What do they mean *just* listening? If they are listening, and thinking about what they are hearing, then they are learning from the exchange. There is also no reason why this has to be an exchange between the teacher and just one pupil. At any point we can draw in someone else by asking them the next question or by requiring them to justify why they agree or disagree with the original response. This brings us to the thorny issue of how to select pupils to answer our questions.

For a while, there was a trend for teachers to reach for a cup of lollipop sticks every time they wanted to ask a question. The idea was to overcome their reliance on pupils putting their hands up to answer, instead selecting a pupil at random by drawing a lollipop stick with their name on it. This is a well-intentioned strategy but it does have its flaws:

- It is often useful to have pupils put their hands up if they feel confident in answering a question. It is a way of quickly gauging who is feeling secure in the topic and who might not be. If you are asking a question about something they have been taught before, you might want to ask the question, have them

---

18 Mark Enser, *Making Every Geography Lesson Count: Six Principles to Support Great Geography Teaching* (Carmarthen: Crown House Publishing, 2019), pp. 117–118.

put their hands up to answer, remind them that they should *all* be able to answer and give them a few seconds longer to really think about it before seeing how many then raise their hand. This encourages the retrieval practice that is so important to the learning process.

- Randomly selecting pupils to answer questions means that we don't target questions where they are needed. I might want to pick one pupil to answer a simple recall question if I know they have struggled with the information in the past, target a more complex question to deepen someone else's understanding, and direct a third to check that another pupil was actually paying attention to the first two questions. Randomly distributing these questions would not work.
- Teachers tend to randomly select the pupil and then ask the question. This means that the rest of the class can switch off before the question is asked and so they are not trying to think of the answer themselves.

One issue that has been created by the desire to demonstrate questioning in the classroom, and to avoid being seen as a teacher who just "tells pupils things", is that teachers find themselves asking "guess what's in my head" questions. These questions are ostensibly asked to establish pupils' prior knowledge, but tend to lead to all kinds of dead ends. Consider the following exchange:

Teacher: Who knows who Catherine Howard was?

Pupil 1: Was she the first woman to fly across the Atlantic?

Teacher: Good guess, but no. We are looking at the Tudors, remember.

Pupil 2: Was she the queen?

Teacher: Well, yes, kind of …

Pupil 2: Yes, that's right. She was that redhead one who sailed the Armada.

Teacher: No, I think you are thinking of Elizabeth I and she didn't …

Pupil 1: That's what I was saying. She was the first person to *sail* the Atlantic.

Teacher: OK, well I'll tell you …

Even if the first pupil had answered correctly, what then? How would the teacher adapt their lesson on this basis? These kinds of questioning exchanges are incredibly common and are symptomatic of a profession who have been told it is wrong to just tell pupils things and that they should work everything out for themselves. Sometimes - often, in fact - we should just tell them in the first instance and ask them questions when they have the knowledge and understanding with which to answer.

Non-teacher input

This chapter has largely been concerned with the idea of an input of new information coming directly from us, as teachers. This is because it is a fundamental part of our job. If the class didn't need our expert input, we could feasibly be replaced by anyone who could simply display task instructions on the board and hand out glue sticks. There is more to teaching than that, and much of this depends on the explanations we give that bring a subject to life.

However, there are other sources of input that we might use in the classroom: other resources that we might select to present new information to pupils on our behalf.

Video

When I started teaching, many moons ago, we had to book a TV which would be wheeled into our classroom ready for the lesson. We would then put on a specially made educational VHS tape that would typically play for 20–30 minutes at a time. Once projectors, interactive whiteboards and YouTube came along, things changed and the way we use video needed to change with it.

One advantage of the educational VHS tape was that it was designed for the school context. The language was pitched at the right level for the target age group and the material was selected to meet a particular objective. Whilst there are many similar clips on platforms like YouTube, it is just as common to see teachers using clips that were not made specifically for the classroom and so therefore need recontextualising for our pupils. We need to make the link explicit between the information they are seeing and the content of the lesson and then direct them to apply the information to a particular task (see Chapter 3 for more on this).

As with teacher explanation, we need to consider the limitations of working memory when pupils are getting an input of new information from a video. They need the same kind of support in terms of making notes or being given a summary of the main points after it has finished. One weakness of using video in place of teacher explanation is that it is much harder to check for understanding throughout. You don't get the same silent cues from body language or puzzled expressions, and there are not the same opportunities for questioning as a natural part of the input. Judicious use of the pause button is needed to make room for questions and to check that everyone is following.

Text

Pupils can also get an input of new information from reading about the subject. As with video, this might come from an age-appropriate educational source, such as a textbook, or from a source designed for a different audience, such as a newspaper article or book extract. These different sources will, of course, need handling differently.

If pupils are reading a piece of extended writing, they might need structures to support their working memory. This could involve providing guidance about what they are looking for before they start reading - for example, by telling them the question they will go on to answer - so that they can pick out and remember just the salient information. It might mean teaching them how to make notes as they read so that they can refer back to these afterwards. It could also involve questioning after the text has been read to check for understanding and support those who struggled.

Experience

Another form of input is direct experience. One reason why we need teacher explanation is because pupils can't experience everything we want them to understand first-hand. That is why we have schools. However, there are many times when pupils can draw on prior first-hand experience or be exposed to novel scenarios to add to their knowledge. The latter often happens during organised field trips.

One thing to remember is that, just as with other forms of input, what pupils are experiencing needs to be put into context by a teacher. In the classroom, we can remove all extraneous information to isolate just the thing we want pupils to think about or observe. This doesn't happen naturally in the field. If we take pupils to follow a river downstream, they may not observe the various factors that affect how it changes over its course. We need to draw their attention to them. All the preceding points about effective input, supporting working memory, storytelling, subject knowledge, etc. still stand - we are now just supporting what we are saying with the biggest prop there is: the world around them.

AVOIDING INPUT PITFALLS

Input is very easy to get wrong. This is one reason - along with poor advice on limiting time spent on explanation - why you often see trainee teachers rushing to get this part of the lesson over with to get the class doing an activity. Standing at the front of the classroom with little more than your voice, a few gestures and a whiteboard pen can feel very exposing. Rushing is the first pitfall and this can be avoided by developing your subject knowledge, so you can speak with more authority on the subject, and by practising your explanation. It can also help to collaborate with more experienced teachers on crafting an explanation.

A second pitfall to be aware of is not maintaining enough momentum. Pupils need to move seamlessly from input to application so that they can apply the ideas that they have just encountered. Thought needs to be given as to how you are going to move from explaining the subject to explaining the task, and then to them doing the task without overloading their working memory and leaving them floundering. (We'll explore this further in Chapter 3.)

One of the biggest pitfalls to avoid is pitching the level of challenge wrong. If your explanation is too simple and feels as though you are going back over what they already know, you risk pupils switching off and missing elements of the new information that you want them to attend to and remember. One way to overcome this problem is to use an intriguing question to introduce something new, before going back over what they need to know to answer it. For example, you might start by explaining that today they are going to look at how different faiths see the relationship between humans and the environment - looking at the question, "Are some religions greener than others?" - before explaining how what they already know might help them. This way they are already re-evaluating their memories in light of the question and thinking about what they already know.

If one problem is moving on too slowly, then the converse risk is jumping too far ahead too rapidly and ending up miles from familiar knowledge. You risk them then having nowhere to hook new ideas onto. They can't make sense of your input in terms of their wider schema. This is why recap is so instrumental to effective input (see Chapter 1).

Effective explanation isn't easy but it does come with deliberate and reflective practice. One useful way to improve your skills is to go through the somewhat uncomfortable experience of recording yourself teach and watching it back from the perspective of a child in the classroom. What was clear? What wasn't? Could you cut out any extraneous information?

This could also be done through a series of peer observations with the aim of creating excellent scripted explanations at the end of the process. One person teaches a lesson with peers observing their explanation and the responses of the class. Everyone feeds back and improves this lesson ready for someone else to teach, which everyone watches before tweaking again. It's a time-consuming process, but one in which the teachers seize back control of their own professional development.

We need to make sure that we are bringing the whole class with us when we are engaged in teacher-talk. It won't work if their attention is elsewhere. We need to make sure that we gain their attention and hold it throughout. We do this by carefully planning our explanation, by purposefully using questioning and through our performance as storytellers who can bring our subject to life.

KEY POINTS

- Teacher input is a vital part of the learning process that has been sadly neglected in recent years.
- One problem with teacher explanation is that we risk overloading working memory. We can overcome this by breaking up our explanation and ensuring that we create notes which pupils can refer back to.
- We can also use the principles of dual coding to support our explanation by including diagrams to illustrate what we are saying.

- People remember stories: if we frame our explanation as a story, it will be more memorable.
- We need to consider how we deliver an explanation. Moving around the room, unless done for a particular reason, is just a distraction.
- Questioning is a vital part of input and different types of questioning need to be used in different ways in order to be effective.
- There are forms of input other than the teacher, but our job is to contextualise this input and help pupils to make sense of it.

REFLECTIONS

- Which elements of your subject do you struggle to explain? What is the difficulty?
- Which analogies do you use in your subject? How do they support your pupils' understanding?
- When might stories be useful in your subject?
- Think back to the last time you delivered an explanation. What did you do to make it effective? What could you have done differently to make it even more memorable?
- Which forms of input, other than teacher-talk, do you use? What are the strengths and drawbacks of each?

CHAPTER 3

APPLICATION

FROM THE CHALKFACE

We had reached the end of a topic about tectonics in which we had focused on the 2004 Boxing Day tsunami. I wanted pupils to understand why the impacts of this event had been so devastating. I had the perfect activity for them - design a newspaper front page about the disaster.

"Sir, how do I make a newspaper front page?"

OK, there was a short diversion whilst I explained the format of a front page.

"Sir, what should I call the paper?"

OK, then followed a slightly longer diversion during which I explained that they could call it whatever they wanted. Having decided upon a name, they painstakingly drew bubble-writing titles.

"Sir, is this the day after? Because don't we need to talk about the problems with the response?"

OK, this provoked an even longer diversion whilst I suggested that they do a front page looking back a year later. Just like actual newspaper front pages don't ...

By the end of the lesson we had some pieces of A3 paper with newspaper names, crossed out dates and wonky lines for columns. There was very little about the tsunami.

I probably should have just asked them to answer the question, "Why were the impacts of the 2004 Boxing Day tsunami so devastating?"

THE IMPORTANCE OF APPLICATION

I remember one of the first sessions I had with my subject tutor on my teacher training course. The group had been discussing the lesson planning process: the difference between objectives and outcomes, differentiation and the need for starters and plenaries. I was feeling increasingly uneasy and worried that I had tuned out and missed something important. "Sorry if this is really obvious," I began tentatively, "but how do we know what they actually need to *do* in a lesson? How do we create the right activity for each lesson?" Blank faces turned my way. "Well," said my tutor airily, "you can get them to do anything. There will be schemes of work in your school to tell you what the pupils should do."

Later on, the tutor shared lots of examples of different tasks. We had sessions on creating card sorts, role playing and setting up self-directed projects. What we never returned to was the purpose of these tasks: what we were asking pupils to do these things for, beyond filling up time on a lesson plan. Over the years, I have found it helpful to stop thinking of the things pupils do in class as "tasks" or "activities"; instead, I think of them as application – the distinction being that there is a focus on them applying what they have been taught. This helps us to move from a culture of doing towards one of learning.

I think that it is in this stage of the lesson, the application, when you will most likely see the implications of teaching like nobody's watching. When they know they are going to be observed, many teachers pull out all the stops. They focus their attention on the task design and try to create something engaging, something that shows pupils working independently. It may involve moving around the room and collecting information from different bases, or sorting out cards, or creating some elaborate project or other.

Watch teachers teaching the rest of the time and you'll see a lot more instances of pupils quietly getting on with answering some questions. Once again, this would suggest that most teachers have worked out what will be effective and efficient in their teaching: they will only distort this practice to satisfy the demands of outside observers.

The aim of application is for pupils to think hard about what they are learning. They are taking the subject matter of your input and applying it in different ways to secure the learning. Daniel Willingham's maxim that "memory is the residue of thought" becomes incredibly significant here.[1] It also highlights the problem with some of the activities carried out in those flashy observation lessons.

If we accept that pupils learn what they think about, we need to look hard at what pupils are really thinking about during our set activities. I can think of one occasion when I asked pupils to make shanty towns - informal housing areas - from cardboard boxes. Every so often I would announce that a disaster had befallen the settlement - such as the government removing buildings, lack of resources or flooding - and I'd come and remove some of their town. The pupils loved the lesson, and so did the observer. The following week I saw the class again. "Think back to last lesson when we were looking at shanty towns," I began. Blank faces looked back at me. "Umm ... can anyone remember what a shanty town is?" One hand hesitantly raised. "Houses built out of cardboard?" "Well, not quite," I replied. "Do you remember how we were looking at the problems people face?" "I remember," one pupil replied. "They struggle to make houses because the glue doesn't stick properly."

Pupils remember what they think about. In this case, they were thinking about making houses from cardboard boxes, and so this is what they remembered. To guide their thinking during this application stage it is important to break tasks down into clear steps, and to ensure that these clear steps involve them thinking about the thing you want them to learn. A better application in this lesson could have involved pupils reading about the lives of different people in shanty towns, identifying the common characteristics and predicting the problems they might face, before reading or watching a second source about those problems to see if they were right. They could then have written a comparison between life in the shanty town and life

1 Willingham, *Why Don't Students Like School?*, p. 54.

elsewhere in the city. This would have involved them applying what they had learnt to a new situation and having to think hard about it, therefore helping retention.

Application also allows you to check on their performance. It is important at this stage to point out that this is not the same as checking on their learning, which will need testing (see Part II). The reason why you see performance during application is because pupils are likely to be working with a range of supports - such as their notes or other resources - and the information will still be fresh in their minds. They are practising so that it eventually becomes learnt.

There is still a lot you can learn from this performance, however. As they are working you can spot misconceptions and common errors creeping into their work, which can then be addressed before they become embedded. You can also get a sense of how effective your input had been and whether something needs to be explained in more depth or with greater clarity. When we teach like nobody's watching, we are always seeking feedback for ourselves and responding to it.

As well as us eliciting feedback from pupils, they can also use this application time to respond to feedback from us. One of the more dispiriting intrusions into lessons in recent years has been so-called directed improvement and reflection time (DIRT). This time is often a too-brief five minutes at the start of the lesson, during which pupils can respond to written comments from the teacher to make improvements to a previous piece of work. The, admittedly sound, idea here is that pupils need to not just receive feedback but act on it. The problem is that they are responding to work that is already completed rather than applying feedback to future pieces of work.

During application we can ask pupils to reflect on recent feedback, show them how to apply it to their current work and then ask them to do so. For example, if a large number of pupils had struggled to comment on a writer's use of language, they could be given examples of where this has been done well, explore what makes it effective, and then complete tasks that involve using this skill - far better than simply correcting their previous errors.

Another important consideration in the application phase of the lesson is how to engineer it to give the pupils a sense of achievement. Lessons often begin with some kind of hook, such as a mystery we want them to solve. "Today we will find out why water is important for life on earth!" or "Today we will explore how J. B.

Priestley's politics influenced his writing!" There is a big overarching question that begs an answer. The process of answering it gives the pupils very visible signs of progress. They can see that they have gone from not knowing where to begin to gathering and piecing together the information they need, but only if they are given the chance to apply what they have learnt.

Some suggest that motivating pupils so that they succeed is misguided; instead, we are better off ensuring that they succeed in order to keep them motivated.[2] We can give them this success through the well-planned application of what they have learnt, leading to a clear outcome of which they can be proud.

APPLICATION IN THE CLASSROOM

Transition

When watching trainee and novice teachers, I can pinpoint in advance when their lesson is most likely to fall apart: it will be in the transition between input and application. That part when the teacher stops explaining and says, "OK, any questions?"

It is at this point when you discover whether your well-crafted explanation has worked and left pupils feeling confident about how to approach the task they have been given. This is why Barak Rosenshine reminds us of the importance of checking for successful knowledge acquisition at this stage: we need to make sure that all pupils have fully understood what we have said before leaving them to apply it independently.[3] If we don't, they will practise with errors or, in a best-case scenario, all raise their hands to ask the same questions as you dart from table to table whilst re-explaining what they need to do.

To prevent this from happening we need to do more than finish our explanation by asking "any questions?" They may not yet know if they have any questions. Instead,

2 Adam Boxer, What is the best way to motivate students in your subject?, *Impact: Journal of the Chartered College of Teaching* 5 (2019): 10–11.

3 Rosenshine, Principles of instruction, 17–18.

we need to ask them questions to check that they know what they are doing. This needs to happen in two stages:

1 Questioning to check understanding of the lesson content.
2 Questioning to check understanding of the task.

We discussed questioning to check understanding of the lesson content in Chapter 2: these are questions that we ask throughout our explanation to ensure that everyone is still following what we are saying. The questions about the task need to check that everyone is very clear on what you want them to do with the new information. We want to avoid making the task itself so complicated that pupils are having to concentrate more on how to complete it than on the thing you actually want them to learn.

This is where teaching like nobody's watching becomes important. When we teach to please outside observers, there is a pressure to make sure that pupils are engaged in some sort of novel task. By its very nature, this means that pupils must first think about the task, before they can even consider applying what they have learnt. This has led to an inordinate number of lessons in which pupils are asked to write a newspaper front page about a topic (whether that be a volcanic eruption, life in the trenches, the death of Romeo and Juliet, or something else). The novelty of the task design means they need to think about their layout, a name for their paper, the price to put on it, a picture to illustrate it and so on (… at some point they may get around to thinking about the volcano, the trenches or the death of the star-crossed lovers).

We need to reduce the extraneous load of the task and instead set questions and activities that are solely focused on exploring the topic at hand. This looks a lot less exciting to an outside observer but is more effective in helping our pupils to learn and more efficient for us in terms of planning. With the task now simplified, the transition into it becomes much smoother. "Answer the question" is a straightforward direction, and saves you unpicking how you want them to set out a double-page newspaper spread complete with grab quotes and illustrations.

The other way in which we can support transition is to support pupils' working memories. As mentioned previously, words are transient. If pupils have been given a lot of information verbally then, even with the best of planning, they may struggle to recall it all when they come to apply it. This is known as the transient information effect. Research by Anne-Marie Singh et al. shows that pupils will struggle to recall large quantities of verbally presented information and will benefit more from having that information in writing.[4]

After spoken input, it is useful to leave key points on the board or compile them on a handout that pupils can refer back to. If the task is more complex than a series of questions, then it's best to display the instructions so that pupils don't have to hold them in their heads.

Modelling

The use of modelling is a key component in successful application. Modelling describes any process whereby we show someone what they should be doing. This might be the correct way to use a piece of equipment in design technology, how to pass a ball in PE or the method for solving a quadratic equation in maths. Sometimes we might simply model how to use subject-specific vocabulary or how to connect different ideas together. It can also be used to show pupils what a written response to a question should look like in your subject.

If, once again, we return to a time when we taught like others were watching, we can see how modelling fell out of favour. Modelling means accepting that the teacher is the expert in the room, who is demonstrating how something should be done. This can sit uneasily with the view that pupils should learn for themselves through discovery, with the teacher simply being on hand to facilitate. If, however, we embrace teaching like nobody's watching, then we can return to using our expertise to help pupils apply what they have learnt. Or "teaching", as it is also known.

We can model through the use of exemplar work. In *An Ethic of Excellence*, Ron Berger explains that he sees one of his roles as a teacher as being an archivist of the excellent work that his pupils have produced.[5] He can then use these examples

4 Anne-Marie Singh, Nadine Marcus and Paul Ayres, The transient information effect: investigating the impact of segmentation on spoken and written text, *Applied Cognitive Psychology* 26(6) (2012): 848–853.
5 Ron Berger, *An Ethic of Excellence: Building a Culture of Craftsmanship with Students* (Portsmouth, NH: Heinemann, 2003).

of excellence to show new classes what they are working towards. It sets the bar of expectation high.

A potential problem with sharing exemplar work as a form of modelling is that it doesn't show pupils *how* to reach this standard. It might look very pretty as a display and it *might* be motivational (although, as we just saw, motivation might follow success rather than lead to it) but it might lead to pupils being no clearer about what they should be doing than they were before. If we use exemplars in this way, it is very important we take the time to unpick them with the class. We need to show them the success criteria we are using when we say that this is excellent work, and then carefully point out how this work meets that criteria.

Exemplars can also be used to good effect as a form of feedback, offered after pupils have completed their own work. If pupils are shown the success criteria, illustrated with examples of that criteria being met, they can then apply this to their own work to make improvements.

Perhaps a better way to approach modelling is to model live, rather than through pre-prepared examples. Modelling live, whether by writing onto the whiteboard or by using a visualiser, means that the teacher can talk through their thought process as they are working. This allows us to explain why we are doing what we are doing. We can narrate as we are writing the model and take breaks to ask pupils to apply what we are saying to their own work. We can also build up live model answers through questioning so that the class creates a model paragraph before continuing independently.

Whether we are using exemplars or modelling live, it is important that pupils continue to refer to these models as they work. Without this reference point, you might find that their work initially follows the high standard of the model but then drifts over time.

Practice vs performance

An important consideration when planning for application is whether we want pupils to practise or perform. Teaching for outside observers can lead us to view pupils' work as a performance, as we need them to demonstrate what they have learnt. This is unfortunate for two reasons. Firstly, research by Nicholas Soderstrom and Robert Bjork suggests that performance is a poor indicator of learning.[6] They explain that learning is about a long-term change in memory and the ability to transfer information into different contexts, whereas performance is a temporary measure of what someone can do at a particular point in time. Pupils may well be able to perform as though they have learnt something when, actually, they have not. This will be especially true if we add lots of supports to help pupils perform (in the form of prompts, support sheets, paragraph structures and guidance notes). This then leads to the second reason why the confusion between practice and performance is so unfortunate: things that make practice more effective in securing long-term learning can also impede performance. Placing an emphasis on performance ignores the importance of practice as part of the learning process.

A common analogy used to illustrate the difference between performance and practice is training to run a marathon. Covering 26.2 miles at race pace is your performance. If you want to run a marathon, you don't practise by going out and running 26.2 miles at this pace day after day; instead, you practise small components that improve your overall ability. You might schedule some sessions to work on speed, but cover little distance, spend time working on your running form, practise hill repeats and throw in some longer runs at a slower speed. You then combine all this on race day to perform well.

In the classroom, we need to consider what our pupils' final performance will involve and then add in small steps of practice that will build towards a successful outcome. If our eventual goal is for them to write an essay on the use of language in *Macbeth*, we need to avoid jumping in with a task that asks them to "Explain how Shakespeare creates a sense of foreboding in *Macbeth*" until they have practised comprehending the text, looking at key scenes, considering the context of the audience and looking at how language is used to create different effects. Once they have practised with these elements, they should then be able to combine them into an effective whole.

It is important to consider the balance of practice and performance because it will affect what you are doing in class. Whilst pupils are practising, you may wish to offer a lot of support to ensure a high success rate and to avoid errors becoming embedded. You may want to scaffold tasks and give plenty of worked examples for them

6 Nicholas C. Soderstrom and Robert A. Bjork, Learning versus performance: an integrative review, *Perspectives on Psychological Science* 10(2) (2015): 176–199.

to refer back to. Our aim here is to make sure that perfect practice makes perfect permanence. During performance, however, we want to see what they can do and may wish to be more judicious with the support we offer by giving pupils a chance to try before we step in to aid or correct.

Differentiation

Differentiation is a topic fraught with complexity and conflicting advice, and it would take a whole book to do it justice. We will confine ourselves here to considering differentiation in the context of teaching like nobody's watching. The first thing we can do is avoid the fads and fashions that plague our classrooms when it comes to differentiating tasks. Two of these in particular have made teaching a lot less efficient and certainly no more effective.

VAK

The first problematic initiative was the fashion for differentiating tasks according to pupils' preferred learning styles. A huge amount of time and energy was spent on this in schools during the early to mid noughties, and the impact lingers today. At this time, it was common for pupils to sit tests to determine their learning style. Often the options were visual, auditory or kinaesthetic (hence the acronym VAK); however, in one school I worked in they went further and identified eight different learning styles, including "musical" and "natural" - crazy days.[7]

Once pupils were tested they were told their preferred learning style and this was displayed on their exercise books (along with their target grades - see Chapter 4 for my ideas on this) and teachers were instructed to plan tasks so that pupils could complete them in their preferred style. This might mean that pupils had the choice between drawing a poster, writing a song or acting out their answer. This would, the theory went, lead to them learning better. It did not.[8]

Although most of the testing apparatus has been dismantled in schools, a vague suggestion that pupils should be able to choose from a range of tasks to suit them

7 See, for example, https://www.skillsyouneed.com/rhubarb/fingerprints-learning-styles.html.
8 See David Didau and Pedro de Bruyckere, Learning myths. In Carl Hendrick and Robin Macpherson (eds), *What Does This Look Like in the Classroom? Bridging the Gap Between Research and Practice* (Woodbridge: John Catt Educational, 2017).

seems to have remained.[9] This is problematic for a number of reasons. Firstly, it is hugely time-consuming for the teacher to create a range of different tasks for each lesson. Given our limited time, we will almost certainly be better off using it for something more effective. Secondly, there is no evidence to suggest that it supports pupils to learn more. There is usually a very good reason why a teacher wants a task completed in a certain way: because it works. If so, that is the way the task should be completed.

Chilli Challenge

The second way of differentiating tasks followed fast on the heels of VAK, and so the chilli challenge was popularised. There are many different permutations, but, broadly, this type of challenge is a response to the insistence that teachers set tasks at a range of difficulties so that pupils can select the one that they feel is most appropriate. There would typically be a "mild" task, a "medium" task and an "extra hot" task. These are often linked to differentiated learning objectives (all will ..., most will ..., some will ...). Sometimes these tasks are linked to different grades so that pupils with a C-grade target would know to do a different task than an A-grade pupil.

Once again, we can see a range of problems with this approach. Firstly, trying to differentiate the task almost always changes it radically. Take this geographical example:

> **Mild** - Describe the location of Uganda.
>
> **Medium** - Explain how the location of Uganda influences the physical geography of the country.
>
> **Extra hot** - Suggest why the location of Uganda may pose difficulties for the people living there.

These tasks certainly do get more complex as they go on, but they also involve pupils practising very different skills and applying very different knowledge. All pupils need to be able to write a good description of location, and it is more difficult than many assume. The medium task involves applying knowledge of

9 Sally Weale, Teachers must ditch the "neuromyth" of learning styles, say scientists, *The Guardian* (13 March 2017). Available at: https://www.theguardian.com/education/2017/mar/13/teachers-neuromyth-learning-styles-scientists-neuroscience-education.

equatorial climate and the extra hot task involves applying knowledge about the barriers to development. Don't all pupils need to practise all of these aspects of application? Is it OK for some of the class to skip this vital practice? If so, why?

Another problem is that a pupil may not be the best person to decide which task they should be completing. That is our job as professionals. Some pupils will always choose what they think is the easiest option - the one that involves thinking less hard, and which therefore leads to less being learnt - whereas other pupils will throw themselves into the most difficult task regardless of whether they have the requisite knowledge or skills to complete it.

Far better, then, to support all pupils to complete the same tasks.

Differentiating support

The book that really changed my approach to differentiating support was Shaun Allison and Andy Tharby's *Making Every Lesson Count*.[10] It helped me to see that it was possible to pitch work at a high level of challenge but then ensure that all pupils were able to rise to it: I didn't need to do what I had always been told to do and differentiate the task itself.

If we aren't going to differentiate the task, we will have to accept the need to differentiate the support we offer to pupils. Sometimes that differentiation is needed because of a physical difficulty in accessing the task - for example, a visual impairment meaning that resources need an increase in font size, and seating plan adjustments or considerations about sensory overload need to be made. We may also need to differentiate due to the variations in working memory capacity that exist between pupils.

Differences in working memory will mean that some pupils will retain a lot more of what you have said than others. It also means that some pupils will find it easier to process information.[11] One way to differentiate support is by giving pupils greater

10 Shaun Allison and Andy Tharby, *Making Every Lesson Count: Six Principles to Support Great Teaching and Learning* (Carmarthen: Crown House Publishing, 2015).
11 Susan E. Gathercole and Tracy Packiam Alloway, *Understanding Working Memory: A Classroom Guide* (London: Harcourt Assessment, 2007). Available at: https://www.mrc-cbu.cam.ac.uk/wp-content/uploads/2013/01/WM-classroom-guide.pdf.

access to material that they may be struggling to hold and manipulate in their working memory or to retrieve from their long-term memory. This could be a list of key words to include in their answer, a diagram showing the process that they are explaining or a paragraph structure to follow.

A potential problem can be created if differentiating resources in advance, as you could give pupils support that they may not actually need, thus enabling them to think less hard than their peers who are making less progress and so do need the resources. A better approach is to provide this support only at the moment of need, as it can then be tailored to the pupil and the context. A great way to do this is through the use of mini whiteboards. You can quickly write down some key words, offer a sentence starter or re-explain something using diagrams or a mind map and then leave the mini whiteboard with the pupil to refer back to whilst they are working.[12]

When we differentiate like nobody's watching we can ensure that we meet the actual needs of the pupils in our classroom rather than trying to make the support obvious to an outside observer. We close the door on fads and fashions and instead do what works for all our pupils.

Group work

When planning for pupils to apply what they have learnt, we need to consider how they will be working. There has, in the recent past, been an assumption that pupils will learn more if they are working in groups: that group work is, in and of itself, a *good thing*. This has meant that teachers have tried to turn any and all activities into group tasks.

There may be times when group work is absolutely appropriate for your class (there are some subjects in which it would be unthinkable not to use group work - for example, team sports in PE) and there is some evidence that "cooperative learning" is an effective way to boost learning.[13] However, it needs to be used judiciously, in the right way at the right time.

---

12 Jules Daulby, All hail! In the inclusive classroom, the mini whiteboard is queen, *Jules Daulby* [blog] (9 December 2018). Available at: https://julesdaulby.com/2018/12/09/all-hail-in-the-inclusive-classroom-the-mini-whiteboard-is-queen/.

13 Robert E. Slavin, Cooperative learning, *Review of Educational Research* 50(2) (1980): 315–342.

If we think back to our four phases of an effective and efficient lesson (recap, input, application and feedback), we can see where group work may or may not have a place. It certainly can't replace the input phase of the lesson. I have been on training courses which have suggested that the pupils are best placed to teach their peers, and that group work will allow this to happen. If they were exploring things that they already know - things that come from everyday life - then this approach might be fine. If, as is arguably more likely, I want them to know about the links between the demographic transition model (DTM) and development, for example, I am probably better placed to teach them.

Group work is also not appropriate in the feedback phase of the lesson, when you want to clearly identify what an individual can and cannot do. Likewise, in the recap phase, group work can mean that an individual does not need to attempt to recall something as others in their group can do the thinking for them. This leaves the application phase.

Even during application, group work can be problematic. We ask pupils to apply what they have learnt to help them consolidate their learning. We want them to think hard about it, apply it to their existing knowledge and so develop their schema (see Chapter 1). This learning is, as Graham Nuthall's book title suggests, hidden inside their heads.[14] Working through a task as a group may add little to the process. Group work seems to work best when there is a high degree of interaction and discussion between different people in the group. This gives pupils a chance to explore their ideas whilst being questioned and challenged on them. Group work then plays a similar role to questioning from the teacher, but with the ability to have several different exploratory dialogues going on at once.

If we think about the last geography example, of the DTM and the link to development, a useful process might be for the teacher to carefully explain the model and its implications before pupils independently decide where a range of countries would be on the model based on the data. Next, they discuss and justify their choices in groups and then, finally, complete an independent task to write up and explain their decisions.

In this way, group work becomes a useful tool with a particular purpose, rather than something done because it will "magically" lead to pupils learning more.

14 Nuthall, *The Hidden Lives of Learners*.

Managing application

Whilst pupils are working, and applying what they have learnt, it can be difficult for the teacher to know what to do with themselves. You sometimes see two extremes. At one end, you have teachers who want to show that they are always working. They buzz around the room, repeating instructions as they go, adding the occasional new piece of information and endlessly intervening. At the other end, you occasionally see teachers who want to show that they are allowing pupils to work independently and so fight every instinct to step in if they see things going awry. They encourage pupils *not* to ask them questions or for help and, instead, try to direct them towards every other possible source of support.

Both extremes of behaviour are often performed to show something to an outside observer - they are behaving in a way that they think they should be behaving - and both are problematic for very different reasons. The problem with the first example is that pupils need to concentrate. If they are to remember what they are thinking about, they need to be thinking hard about what they are doing. We also risk increasing the cognitive load with every interruption. In fact, it might be better to view the teacher's role during pupil application as one of reducing interruptions. This could include:

- Ensuring that pupils have everything they need to complete a task before they begin - both in terms of the instructions for the task and secure knowledge with which to complete it.
- Insisting that pupils work in silence during independent work. If they have already had the chance to discuss their ideas, and have everything they need to complete the task, there really shouldn't be any need for them to talk.
- Keeping the classroom door open - providing the corridor is quiet - so that any visitors can come in with minimal disruption. If there is noise elsewhere, then close the door but ask visitors to knock and wait. Put learning first.
- Remove distractions from the front of the class. There is sometimes encouragement for teachers to fill their room with displays, but these can easily draw attention (if they don't, you have to wonder what they are for anyway). This can be particularly important for pupils with autism spectrum disorder

(ASD), who may suffer from sensory overload and struggle to know where to focus when their attention is divided.[15]

- Insist that mobile phones and other devices are well out of reach unless being used for the task. Few things draw focus as effectively as a notification suddenly popping up on a screen.

What we are aiming for is an atmosphere of studious calm in which pupils can focus on the work in front of them. If in doubt, imagine that you are trying to concentrate on reading and understanding a really dense text for an important assignment. Ask yourself, "Would this help me to work?" If it wouldn't help you, don't inflict it on them.

The second type of behaviour – trying to show how independent the class are and leaving them to get on with tasks, even if they ask for help – has its own problems. Although this may seem extreme, it is something that I have been encouraged to do, and I still see teachers being given this advice. A common suggestion is to use the four Bs: brain, book, buddy, boss. In other words, before asking the expert in the room (you, the teacher) for help, pupils should think about it, check their book in case the answer was there all along, and disturb the person next to them to ask for help.

On the face of it, this isn't terrible advice (well, apart from the distracting your neighbour part). Sometimes pupils are too quick to ask for help and just need to think a bit first. Other times, they really don't. They are asking because they need your guidance as the best person in the room to get it from. It is possible that the answer is in their book, but if they have genuinely been learning rather than just working, it should be in their head by now. What we are seeing here is another example of good teaching (i.e. saying to pupils "think about it first") becoming distorted as school policy. If we actively discourage pupils from asking for help when they are running into difficulty, we increase the chance of them embedding errors in their work. It is hard enough to keep a check on misconceptions when pupils are unaware of them, so why would we want to let them include errors they are pretty sure they are making?

15 Keith McAllister, The ASD Friendly Classroom – Design Complexity, Challenge and Characteristics (2010). Available at: https://www.researchgate.net/profile/Keith_Mcallister/publication/267684638_The_ASD_Friendly_Classroom_-_Design_Complexity_Challenge_and_Characteristics/links/54942cd30cf2e572fa53a8cb/The-ASD-Friendly-Classroom-Design-Complexity-Challenge-and-Characteristics.pdf.

As with so many things, it comes down to knowing the pupils in your class. Some will need you to step back and leave them to it and others will need more monitoring and support. This is just another reason why we need to teach like nobody's watching and do what works best for our pupils in that moment.

AVOIDING APPLICATION PITFALLS

One problem with this model of input and application is getting the balance right between the two. Too much input before too little application can mean that much of the new information is lost as pupils have had no chance to do anything with it. If too little input is followed by too much application, then we could be asking them to do things they just don't yet have the knowledge to do successfully. A lot of this will depend on your subject. In maths, pupils will develop fluency by being shown how to do something and then doing plenty of practice with that same thing. In a subject like history, there are fewer occasions when developing fluency in a specific skill in this way would be appropriate.

One way to avoid this pitfall is to consider everything you have included in the input phase (from your own explanation, written sources, video clips, artefacts, etc.) and ask yourself whether pupils have had the chance to use it all in their own work. If they haven't, you may need to take some elements out or change the tasks so that they are using everything in some way.

Likewise, look at what you are asking them to do. Consider the perfect piece of work you would like them to produce, and consider how and where you are expecting them to find the information they will need. If you are hoping that they will magic things up, you may need to go back to your input to include it, or change the task to remove its inclusion until a later date.

One concern that teachers sometimes have when moving from an approach that involves creating elaborate, seemingly engaging activities to an approach that requires shorter and more focused tasks is that the pupils will find lessons boring and that each lesson will be the same as the one before. But we have to remember that we see a pupil's day only though our own eyes when they arrive in our classroom. In a typical day, your pupil may have started with a drama lesson, working in groups on a performance, then spent time in English reading and annotating poetry in pairs, then gone to geography to learn all about that fascinating DTM, then off to science to explore the structure of cells before finishing the day with maths, and learning something completely new about geometry. Even if each lesson utilised the principles outlined here, the pupil would still experience a very varied day.

Humans in general - and children in particular - are naturally curious creatures and we enjoy learning things. There is something satisfying about solving a problem and reaching an answer to a question. This is where the real fun lies, not in the superficial activity that surrounds the learning. Planning "fun" activities tends to lead to disappointment for everyone.

KEY POINTS

- Plan tasks that require pupils to think hard about what they have just learnt and apply it to a question.
- Build smaller tasks up until pupils can answer bigger, more satisfying questions.
- Try to create tasks that require pupils to link lessons together and apply what they have learnt in previous topics to what they are currently learning about.
- Ensure that pupils have secure knowledge before they start working. You want them to practise perfectly and not embed errors.
- Also ensure that they have fully understood the task before they start working.
- Differentiate at the point of need by adapting the amount of support that pupils can access to complete the task, rather than by setting different work for them.
- Model your expectations clearly. Unpick any examples you give and clearly show how they link to the success criteria. Ask pupils to apply these models to their own work.
- Consider the purpose of group work - don't assume that working in a group always leads to more being learnt. The opposite will often be the case.
- Remove distractions when pupils are working.

REFLECTIONS

- Is your classroom a calm working environment? Imagine you were trying to mark a complex essay as pupils were working independently - would this be easy to do? What would be the barriers and how could you remove them?
- What is the purpose of the lessons you are teaching? What are you hoping your pupils will be able to do by the end (beyond passing an exam)?
- Do your pupils know what an excellent piece of work looks like in your subject? How do they know? Does their own work look like this? If not, why not?
- Consider the activities you asked pupils to complete in the last lesson you taught:
  - What did they need to know in order to complete the activities?
  - Where did this information come from?
  - Did they need to use any knowledge or skills from previous lessons?
  - Were the activities focused on the thing they needed to learn, or would they have been thinking more about the structure of the activity itself?

CHAPTER 4

FEEDBACK

FROM THE CHALKFACE

I remember one day, towards the end of my NQT year, my head of department coming to see me as I sat planning. She was in a bit of a panic. "Your books!" she exclaimed. "They haven't been marked for four weeks and the SLT are going to do a book check tomorrow!" The idea of the senior leadership team (SLT) checking books was still something very new and scary, part of the brave new world of increased accountability. My planning was hurled aside so I could spend the afternoon and evening marking work that was weeks old, writing in comments like, "You need to develop your point" that no pupil would ever read, or be able to do anything with even if they had. Book after book I worked through in a frenzy, in order to show an assistant head teacher that they had been marked: not to show that my feedback was having an impact or that progress was being made, but that there was ink on the page.

A week later we got the feedback from this book check. My marking had been held up as an example of good practice and, they went on to say, helped to explain the high quality of work my pupils were producing. I remember thinking then, there has to be more to teaching than this.

WHY DO WE GIVE FEEDBACK?

High workload is the number one reason for teachers leaving the profession, and the number one cause of this workload? Marking. A 2016 *Guardian* survey found that 82% of teachers described their workload as unmanageable, with 73% saying that it was having an impact on their physical health. Nearly half of respondents said that they were thinking of leaving the profession within five years.[1] The *Evening Standard* even reported that teachers are opting to work part-time in order to get their marking done.[2] The image of the harried teacher, slumped over their classroom desk late into the evening, or loading bags of books into the boot of their car on a Friday afternoon, seems to be etched into our collective imagination. How did it get this way?

When I first started teaching there was still the assumption that most teachers were just marking to make corrections and to give grades, but this would quickly change. Over the last decade or so we have seen the following strategies arrive and make their mark, often under the catch-all phrase "assessment for learning" (AfL):[3]

- **Writing improvement targets on pupils' work.** Targets were, at first, linked to their predicted grades, but with no expectation that pupils would do anything to improve their work based on the targets. They were often very vague and based on national curriculum levels. You'd see a lot of "Explain your answer" and "Add more evidence" without any real guidance provided on how to *do* these things.
- **Marking policies.** These policies spelt out how often books would be marked. Not what would be marked, or why, just how often. There are still schools that make claims like, "Books will be marked every two weeks." Teachers of non-core subjects might have 14 classes on their timetable. That means marking a set of books every day and marking one lesson's worth of material a

1 Liz Lightfoot, Nearly half of England's teachers plan to leave in next five years, *The Guardian* (22 March 2016). Available at: https://www.theguardian.com/education/2016/mar/22/teachers-plan-leave-five-years-survey-workload-england.

2 Hatty Collier, Teachers "opting to work part-time to finish marking on days off", *Evening Standard* (3 April 2016). Available at: http://www.standard.co.uk/news/education/teachers-opting-to-work-parttime-to-finish-marking-on-days-off-a3506086.html.

3 For a discussion on how AfL has been misused and abused see Daisy Christodoulou, *Making Good Progress: The Future of Assessment for Learning* (Oxford: Oxford University Press, 2017).

time. Others might have far fewer classes but see them every day, so when they sit down to mark, they are marking ten lessons' worth of material. If the policy doesn't seem to care about the workload created, it is because it doesn't. It just wants the books marked.

- **Dialogic marking.** The teacher would mark the books, the pupils would respond, the teacher would re-mark the work. It was often claimed that this was something that Ofsted wanted, which led to Sean Harford - their national director of education - issuing a number of "myth buster" statements. One of which was that Ofsted did not require or favour any particular approach to marking and feedback.[4]
- **Coloured pens.** I suspect that there are members of SLTs around the country with shares in green ink manufacturing. Marking policies started specifying that teachers would mark in one colour, pupils would respond in another, the teacher would use a third for re-marking, there would be a fourth for peer marking ... and on and on it went. (I actually once heard a teacher say, "I took my books home to mark but couldn't find a green pen so I couldn't mark them.")

The problem with many of these approaches is that they were designed not because they are an effective way to improve progress, but for an audience: because the policy-makers believed that it was "what Ofsted wanted", or that pupil voice showed that they appreciated it, or that parents wanted it. It had nothing to do with the needs of pupils or teachers.

The Department for Education's workload review group concluded that:

> Marking has evolved into an unhelpful burden for teachers, when the time it takes is not repaid in positive impact on pupils' progress. This is frequently because it is serving a different purpose such as demonstrating teacher performance or to satisfy the requirements of other, mainly adult, audiences.[5]

4 Ofsted, Ofsted Inspection - Clarification for Schools (guidance to accompany *School Inspection Handbook*. Ref: 150066, September 2018). Available at: https://www.gov.uk/government/publications/school-inspection-handbook-from-september-2015.

5 Department for Education, *Eliminating Unnecessary Workload Around Marking: Report of the Independent Teacher Workload Review Group* (March 2016), p. 6. Available at: https://www.gov.uk/government/publications/reducing-teacher-workload-marking-policy-review-group-report.

This statement cuts to the core purpose of this book. The problem with marking is that we do it because we are worried about who might be watching, not because of the impact we think it will have on learning. This outlook isn't leading to effective or efficient practice.

A second problem is that we are essentially conflating marking and feedback in these kinds of policies. Feedback is a vitally important part of learning; indeed, it is difficult to imagine learning how to do anything without some form of feedback about whether you are doing it right. We seek feedback constantly: we taste our sauce as we are cooking to check whether we need more seasoning, we ask a friend to look over an important letter before we send it, we record data when we are running to look for improvement. Marking, though, is just one feedback tool and often the least efficient one in the kit.

In their myth-busting guidance, Ofsted say that:

> Ofsted recognises that marking and feedback to pupils, both written and oral, are important aspects of assessment. However, Ofsted does not expect to see any specific frequency, type or volume of marking and feedback; these are for the school to decide through its assessment policy. Marking and feedback should be consistent with that policy, which may cater for different subjects and different age groups of pupils in different ways, in order to be *effective and efficient* in promoting learning.[6]

Let's stop the marking madness and start again. If nobody was watching, how would you give feedback? What would be in your own feedback policy?

We need to start by reminding ourselves that the original purpose of feedback is twofold:

1. We want to *get* feedback so that we know what pupils know and can do.
2. We want to *give* feedback so that we can tell pupils what they need to do to improve.

6 Ofsted, Ofsted Inspection – Clarification for Schools, p. 2. My italics for emphasis.

Once we have established that the purpose is this simple, we can largely throw away the red (or green) pen and focus on more effective and efficient ways of giving and getting this information.

FEEDBACK IN THE CLASSROOM

The image of a teacher slumped over piles of exercise books belongs to another age: one in which we taught for an audience other than our pupils. Giving feedback begins in the classroom and can largely remain there. It is an intrinsic part of teaching, rather than something that happens when the class have left and you remain, pen in hand. If feedback were left up to teachers, it would look very different. It would focus on effective ways of getting and giving the information we need, as quickly and efficiently as possible. Putting this into practice involves three steps: reducing the need, reducing the time spent and making every word count.

Step one - reduce the need

Imagine that every piece of work that a pupil handed to you was excellent - everything they should or could produce. What would that do to your marking load? Let's see how close we can get to that ideal.

Careful instruction

The first step in reducing the need for marking is to make sure that pupils make fewer mistakes in the first place. If you are teaching a class how to use six-figure grid references and half the class have written the northing and easting the wrong way round, you could find yourself having to write, "You have written the northing and easting the wrong way round" in 15 books (I have just had to write it twice and I am bored of doing so already). If your explanation is clear enough to begin with, there is no reason for this error to occur. (Even if it does, you don't need to write the correction in every book - and we'll see why shortly.) It is amazing how much time can be spent on correcting these kinds of errors. The same goes for "Always write in full sentences" and "Explain your answer" - make your expectations clear in each lesson and the need to mark is immediately reduced.

Barak Rosenshine suggests that teachers need to achieve a high success rate during instruction so that pupils do not embed errors in their work. He argues that:

> If the practice does not have a high success level, there is a chance that students are practicing and learning errors. Once errors have been learned, they are very difficult to overcome.[7]

One way to ensure that this happens is to carefully chunk lessons so that pupils are given precise instructions on the very next activity they need to complete. In this way, their working memory isn't overloaded (see Chapter 2).

Success criteria

The second way in which we can reduce the need for marking is to share the success criteria and instruct pupils to use it to check their own work before they hand it in. Some of these criteria will be the same for all tasks and some will be highly specific. Generic criteria might include things like:

- ✓ Use a ruler and a pencil to draw a graph.
- ✓ Check your answer with a neighbour. If it is different, work out why.
- ✓ Use the term "sustainable" when justifying decisions.
- ✓ Check you have used the correct homophone (e.g. their, there, they're).

A more task-orientated list might look more like this:

- ✓ Use data from the climate graph.
- ✓ Refer to the impacts of the wet monsoon on at least three groups of people.
- ✓ Show you understand that the rain moves north over time.

These are the types of errors that teachers have corrected and commented on time after time, and it just isn't efficient. There is even some evidence that providing this kind of feedback could be harmful as it creates a dependency. Pupils come to expect correction from the teacher, rather than developing the ability to proofread

7 Rosenshine, Principles of instruction, 17.

and edit. This is the type of thing a successful pupil should be able to do for themselves, exercising what John Hattie and Helen Timperley call self-regulation.[8] Pupils will have to do this in their exams, so it's best they learn how as early as possible.

Step two – reduce time spent

However much you reduce the need for marking, there will come a point when you need to look at your pupils' work and give them feedback on how to improve. However, it still doesn't have to mean wearily sifting through a pile of books and scribbling comments in each. There are more effective and efficient methods.

Verbal feedback

One of the most effective ways of giving feedback is to do so verbally. Verbal feedback is far more immediate than written feedback and your exact meaning can be clarified for the pupil. No more time wasted whilst they ponder, "Just what did sir mean by 'Add more detail'?"

There are two different approaches to verbal feedback.

1. For simple tasks in which the mistake you have spotted is largely procedural, give the feedback as pupils are doing the work. Circulate the room and check that their work is correct. Have they used the right type of graph to display that data? Have they started the sentence properly? Have they explained and justified their point before moving on? Some teachers prefer to put a dot in the margin when they spot an error, then the pupils need to look for and correct it; others like to write the correction in so that pupils can refer back to the information. You are trying to pick up on errors before they become embedded – before practice makes not perfect but permanent.
2. For feedback that tells pupils how to move on in their learning, it is more effective to wait until they have completed a few pieces of work and had the time to reflect. When the class are working on an independent task for a significant amount of time, find somewhere unobtrusive to sit and call up pupils, one at a time, with their books to talk through their work. What are they

8 John Hattie and Helen Timperley, The power of feedback, *Review of Educational Research* 77(1) (2007): 81–112.

doing well? What needs to be improved? Write comments in their book as you go and use homework to make any changes or improvements. If you can see four pupils each lesson, you should be able to give every pupil some very effective, meaningful feedback each term.

There was a trend for a while for verbal feedback stamps. The idea was that when you gave feedback verbally, you'd stamp their work so that an inspector or observer would know that it had happened. Don't do this. Remember that we are teaching like nobody's watching.

Whole-class feedback

Of course, it isn't always possible or desirable to give feedback live: sometimes you want to take a more detailed look at a pupil's work, or look at everyone's work at the same time. This will often be the case with assessments or practice exam papers.

Picture the scene. The smell of mulled wine, the John Lewis advert on TV, houses lit up with decorations; it can only mean one thing. Yes, it is mock exam season.

In the past, I would not only mark the papers but cover them with annotation to give feedback to each individual pupil. The next lesson, I would give out the papers and talk through the common mistakes and points from the examiner's report (i.e. the exact same information I had decorated their papers with) before they redrafted their answers to the questions they had done badly on. Then those papers would be gathered in to collect dust on a shelf and, perhaps, be handed back as a reminder before the final exams.

Now I spend a lot less time marking and a lot more time making sure that what I do makes a difference to the pupils. The process now looks like this:

1 Mark the papers but just write the mark for each question. Don't write any other annotation. Make a note of common errors and any thoughts about each question that you want to feed back to pupils.

2 In the next lesson they get their papers back - without the grade because, firstly, all they fixate on is this grade and nothing else[9] and, secondly, if they have done very well you want them to get the feedback without a sense of complacency setting in. Talk through each question and draw their attention to common mistakes that were made. As you go through, *they* can annotate their papers.
3 They can then redraft answers that they didn't do well on.
4 The following lesson, look at a selection of answers to questions on which they performed poorly as a class and carry out some comparative judgement work to evaluate what makes a good answer.
5 Create some exemplar answers to similar questions for them to critique (see Chapter 3).
6 Then set them some different exam questions in areas which they were weak on to see if they can show improvement.

Notice that they are now working much harder than you are: a sign that you are getting it right. And, of course, this doesn't only work for exam papers. You can give effective whole-class feedback on any work. In fact, if you are in a rush, you don't even need to look at every book every time. Pick a sample of books from the class and make a note of the feedback that you would give them. Everyone can then look at their work to see if they have made the same errors and, if so, correct them. If your sample shows that the same error keeps occurring, it is a sign that it will probably be more efficient to reteach the material than to give each pupil feedback about it.

Quiz

If you want feedback on what pupils have learnt, then there is a temptation to look at their classwork and conclude that if they have successfully completed the work then they have learnt what you intended. Unfortunately, this isn't necessarily the case. They may be mimicking what they have just heard, copying from a book or

9 There is some research to support this idea that pupils, having seen their grade, then ignore further feedback. See Ruth Butler, Enhancing and undermining intrinsic motivation: the effect of task-involving and ego-involving evaluation on interest and performance, *British Journal of Educational Psychology* 58(1) (1988): 1-14.

guessing. Most of their classwork, in most subjects, tells you very little about the learning that has taken place.

If you want feedback on what they have learnt in a particular lesson, you are far better off waiting a few days (in many subjects that will probably be the next lesson) and starting with a short quiz. This takes advantage of the spacing effect discussed in Chapter 1. Put a few simple questions on one slide and the answers on the next so they can mark their own. You can then either record their score to see if they are improving over time, or quickly check who got each question right to find particular areas that need reteaching. Repeat the quiz a few weeks later to see what has stuck.

Step three - make every word count

Every so often, I'll find that marking and annotating a piece of work is the most effective way of giving feedback. Usually this is because I go to look through a pile of books and find that, on this occasion, pupils have made very different errors that need very different feedback, or because I want to look at some work over the holidays and know I won't remember my verbal feedback in enough detail.

Whatever the reason, if I am going to spend my time marking books, I want to be sure that every moment spent, and every word written, counts.

Mark with a purpose

One problem with many marking policies I have seen is that they focus on how often books should be marked, rather than on any deeper purpose of the marking. The presence of some red (or green, purple, lilac or maroon) ink on the page becomes the purpose. This leads to teachers engaging in "back marking": trawling through books to mark work that was completed several weeks previously and that pupils will likely never look at again. Never mark a piece of work without a clear purpose. Ask yourself, what am I doing this for? How will this help someone make progress?

Be wary of corrections

When I started teaching, it was expected that any errors in spelling or grammar would be corrected. In practice, this meant some pupils getting work back with every word crossed out and the correct spelling written above it. I am not sure this has ever helped anyone improve their literacy.

If self-regulation is the ultimate aim of feedback, then we want to avoid making the corrections ourselves. Instead, highlight errors and give pupils time to work out what the mistake is and how to correct it themselves. Over time, move on to the dot marking method that I mentioned on page 81. This works best with the types of errors that occur due to laziness or hurried work. Few pupils don't *know* that the first letter of a new sentence should be a capital letter, and they should be able to find these errors themselves. The kinds of errors you do need to correct are ones that come from genuine misconceptions. Many pupils miss the letter N in environment, for example. It doesn't matter how long you give them to find it, they are unlikely to identify a misspelling of that word.

Specific improvements

I dread to think how many times, early on in my teaching career, I wrote "write in more detail" as a target. The problem with such "targets" is that the only sensible response a pupil can make is, "Well, I would write in more detail if I knew how to." If they had written a poor piece of work out of laziness, they should probably just be told to redo it to the best of their ability. In most cases though, either the level of detail needed has not been clear or they do not have enough knowledge about the subject to add more detail.

Conversely, it can be problematic if the comments suggest improvements that are *too* specific: things that would apply to this piece of work only, but not anywhere else. These are useful in the given context, but pupils are not able to generalise from these sorts of comments, which could include things like:

- Include the actual death toll of the Nepal earthquake.
- Refine your definition of photosynthesis.
- Mention the first time the writer suggests that this character may be the villain.

Reminders of things a pupil should always do when faced with this kind of task are more useful as targets. Examples could include:

✓ Support your point with a quote – for example …

✓ Start your paragraph with your point, not with a case study.

✓ Refer to a range of sources - for example ...

They then need time to make these improvements. This could be by redrafting this particular piece of work or, perhaps more usefully, by attempting a second task in which the same targets would apply. This helps them to see that the targets don't only apply to one question but are areas to develop throughout their work.

PEDAGOGY VS PLENARY

Finally, we need to think about when in a lesson we as teachers *get* feedback from our pupils about what they have understood. There was a time, and in many schools it may still be the case, when there was an expectation that lessons would end with a "plenary" session in which understanding could be checked. This needed to be done so that outside observers could have learning demonstrated to them.

The problem is that the end of the lesson is the worst possible time to discover what pupils have and have not learnt and/or understood. Firstly, we are still quite close to the point when there has been some kind of input. When you get a response from a pupil at the end of the lesson, it can be very hard to determine if they have really understood it or whether you are simply getting mimicry of the content you have just delivered. Will they be able to give this answer in a few days' time? You are probably better off waiting and asking then.

Secondly, what are you going to do if your plenary session reveals that pupils haven't understood something or, even worse, have *misunderstood* something? Are you going to let them walk out the door with those misconceptions articulated but not addressed? It would make more sense to get this feedback from them at a point when you can do something about it. Not at the end of a lesson.

I would suggest that, in many cases, end-of-lesson plenaries are an example of practice that developed to meet the needs of outside observers and that, if we are going to teach like nobody's watching, we can find a better time and way to get the information we need.

AVOIDING FEEDBACK PITFALLS

There can be a temptation, when the scales fall from our eyes, to allow our zealous move away from marking to leave us without other forms of feedback in place. Before we throw away our red pens, we do need to consider how we are going to replace marking with a more effective and efficient form of feedback. We also need to be careful that the replacement truly is more efficient. Whole-class feedback, as we saw, is an excellent tool and one that is increasingly being adopted in school feedback policies. Many of these schools are introducing templates that teachers can complete to record the feedback they wish to give to the class. Whilst a good idea in principle, a potential pitfall can be that filling in the template takes more time than writing comments in pupils' books. There is a real concern that these templates just become a new way of collecting evidence of feedback for outside observers.

We also need to keep in mind the role that feedback plays on the attitudes and motivations of our pupils. If they are used to receiving lots of written comments in their books, and then this stops, will they feel as though their work is not getting the attention it deserves? We need to be very clear with our pupils when feedback is occurring, assuring them that we are still looking at their work and considering it carefully. They also need to know that we are noticing when work is not completed, or not completed to the best of their ability. This can be achieved through the kind of verbal feedback discussed in this chapter or through the sharing of excellent work during whole-class feedback.

KEY POINTS

- Marking is not the only form of feedback. In fact, it is often not even the most effective form of feedback.
- Feedback should be used to learn what pupils know and tell them how to improve.
- The ultimate aim of feedback should be for pupils to become self-regulating. Encourage them to proofread and look for errors themselves.

- Verbal feedback means that pupils can ask for clarification. This makes it much more useful than written feedback.
- If you are giving written feedback, make the targets specific enough to be acted on but not so specific that they would only ever apply to this exact question.

REFLECTIONS

- Think about a topic you are currently teaching. What common errors do you find?
- What comments do you often give pupils as feedback? What improvements do you see afterwards?
- How much feedback do you do because you think your pupils will benefit? How much do you do because you think you must?
- Think about the last lesson you taught. What feedback did you give during the lesson? Is feedback an intrinsic part of your teaching?
- If you never marked another piece of work again, what difference do you think it would make?

PART II
THE CURRICULUM

INTRODUCTION TO PART II

In the lesson, as we have just seen in Part I, is probably where the individual teacher has the most power to take back control of their professional practice, but it is the curriculum that really influences the educational experience of all those children who pass through the school for years to come. These decisions are often taken at a department level – whereas the lesson is delivered at an individual level – but this doesn't mean that everything needs to, or should, fall on heads of department. As professionals we need to work collaboratively within our subject areas to ensure that we create the excellent curriculum our pupils deserve.

Teachers sometimes overlook just how much power they have over what they teach in their classrooms. Even if they are following the national curriculum at Key Stages 1–3 and exam specifications at GCSE and A level, there is still a huge number of decisions that are left to schools about what to teach and when to teach it. Some multi-academy trusts (MATs) are attempting to impose ready-made schemes of work and resources on all schools in their group, but even in those instances there are opportunities to emphasise what you feel matters, to distort, change and hopefully improve that which is given from on high. We can still teach what we want, like nobody's watching.

One reason why we can do so is because there is a difference between the formal curriculum (that which is given to us to follow) and the enacted curriculum (that which is taught in class). The formal curriculum might tell me that in Key Stage 3 I need to teach a region in Africa, but it doesn't tell me which one. It only gives a brief overview of expected content (the major climate types, ecosystems, countries, etc.) but does not detail what to teach about them. Most importantly, the formal curriculum rarely spells out in any detail *why* we are teaching these things. This is the first area of decision making for the teacher, from which all else should flow.

The purpose of your curriculum will depend on how you see the purpose of education as a whole. If you believe, as some do, that a major function of school is to prepare pupils for the world of work then your curriculum decisions will reflect that. Your regional study of Africa might focus on the so-called lion economies of east Africa and the business opportunities found there. An English curriculum might emphasise the so-called functional skills of literacy rather than deep studies of literature. The history curriculum might emphasise the transferable skills that could be of use to future employers.

If, on the other hand, you see your curriculum's purpose as revolving more around developing a social conscience in your children then your schemes of work will reflect this. That geography unit could focus on the controversial role that aid plays in development of the countries in the Sahel region. The English curriculum could select texts that explore poverty and exploitation, and in history there is an opportunity to emphasise the moral lessons from the past when looking at slavery or the Holocaust.

These two curriculum intentions were handed down to staff in schools I have worked in over the years. They are what many people outside of education - and many inside - want from schools, and I laboured to produce a curriculum that matched their intentions. This was not, however, what I wanted from the curriculum: it was planned for outside observers and their desires.

My intention when enacting the curriculum is now clear: I want to take what has been learnt over 10,000 years of recorded human history and pass on what I can to the next generation. I see this as their inheritance, their birthright. At the same time, I want to ensure that they know enough about the world and how it works to make sense of anything else they come across by being able to relate it to what they already know. I would like to think that some of my pupils will go on to add to this body of knowledge that will, in turn, be passed on in the future.

Now that my curriculum intention is clear, it is much easier to make decisions about what to teach. There is a clear and transparent purpose behind my programme of study and schemes of work that was lacking when I tried instead to please others and to reconcile competing demands.

As well as discussing the curriculum as it is planned for and enacted in our classrooms, this part will discuss the wider curriculum of what is learnt outside of the classroom and how we assess what has been learnt. Finally, it will look at the role of departmental meetings and how this time can be better used to support teachers in achieving the aim of teaching like nobody's watching.

CHAPTER 5

THE PROGRAMME OF STUDY

When teachers talk about "the curriculum" they are likely to be referring to the programme of study - the long-term plan of what gets taught and when - in their subject. These long-term plans, along with the medium-term plans of schemes of work for individual topics, are the subject of this chapter and follow on from the discussion of lesson planning in Part I.

The forms of these long- and medium-term plans vary enormously from school to school and between departments within a school. Some programmes of study are no more than a list of topics in the order in which they will be taught, and schemes of work no more than a list of lesson objectives that each teacher will need to cover. Others have programmes of study that seek to give a clear rationale about what is being taught when and why, and schemes of work that contain individual, fully resourced lessons for everyone in the department to use.

However much detail you decide to include in the written document which spells out your plans, this chapter will go through some important considerations for you to evaluate. Decisions regarding the structure of the curriculum matter and shouldn't be left up to whim and chance. In recent years, I have come across the following examples of curriculum planning gone badly wrong:

- Someone asking for some ideas for topics for their Year 8 scheme of work because they felt they were going to finish everything too soon.
- English departments in which each class studies whichever text the teacher could get hold of from the stock cupboard that term.

- Departments of option subjects putting what they view as their most "exciting" topics at the point at which pupils in Key Stage 3 would be choosing their GCSEs.
- Teaching the geography of sport to one class because there were a lot of disaffected boys in it, whilst the other classes studied ecosystems.

What these examples have in common is that decisions were made due to expediency, cost or confusion, rather than for any educational reason. They all view the curriculum as a collection of topics that can be drawn out of a hat and taught in any order, which is not the case.

The word curriculum is derived from the Latin word for the route of a race, a course, a journey - and our curriculum should be similar. It is the journey you are taking your pupils on and, as with any journey, you will all benefit from having a well-thought-out map. This map is your programme of study.

PREVIOUS KNOWLEDGE

Most journeys have a beginning. You are at your starting point, you identify your path, and off you go. One thing that complicates the journey that you are taking your pupils on is that whilst you have the map of where you want your pupils to go, they are all starting from different points and will take different routes to get there. They might tell us that they are keeping up with us but, in reality, they are completely lost. If we aren't careful, we can go striding off down the road thinking that we are taking the group with us only to find that someone has either been left behind or has run off ahead.

We need to think very carefully about what pupils already know, understand and can do and then consider what this means for the curriculum. In part, this will come down to the subject and key stage you teach. A Year 7 English teacher might have a very good idea about what has been covered previously in terms of language, if only due to the presence of external exams in this area. The same is true for maths. A teacher in a foundation subject, though, may have very little idea.

Previous reports into the teaching of foundation subjects, such as geography, reveal that there is a huge amount of variation in what has been covered at Key Stage 2.[1] It varies not only due to the priorities of the school but also to the interests of the individual teacher. So, what is a teacher to do?

One option is to try to find out everything your pupils already know about your subject. Some schools do this by starting the year with some sort of "baseline" test that they hope will tell them pupils' starting abilities in the subject. This will only tell you what they know about what you ask about, however – and trying to cover every topic would soon become unmanageable.

Another option is to do absolutely nothing. You are teaching like nobody's watching, and although it might be useful to know what pupils already know, we might have to accept that not everything that would be useful is actually possible. Even if you contacted each pupil's feeder school and discovered what was on their programme of study for your subject, this wouldn't actually tell you what they have learnt, just what they have done. The problem with this approach is that you could find yourself either reteaching the entire Key Stage 1 and 2 curriculum to be sure they know what you need them to know, or continuing on with your programme of study despite obvious gaps in their knowledge.

A better option is likely to be somewhere in-between those two extremes. Be aware of anything you are teaching that requires pupils to use knowledge which you believe they already have, and check that they have the knowledge before you begin the topic. This could easily be achieved through a recap quiz at the start of a lesson (as we saw in Chapter 1), with opportunities to address any misconceptions or gaps that the quiz reveals before moving on to what you want to teach.

Of course, when you expect previous knowledge to have been gained during their time in your own school, you would hope to be on a firmer footing. However, you still have to keep in mind that having done something isn't the same as having learnt and retained it. This is one reason why it is useful to have an assessment model that tracks the detail of what has been learnt, rather than something as ephemeral as "progress" (we'll see what this looks like in Chapter 7).

---

1 Simon Catling, Rachel Bowles, John Halocha, Fran Martin and Steve Rawlinson, The state of geography in English primary schools, *Geography* 92(2) (2007): 118–136.

STARTING FROM SCRATCH

One issue with curriculum design is that it frequently begins with existing content. Most programmes of study evolve over the years with heads of department and teachers adding new topics, taking some away and altering existing lessons. Whilst this is completely understandable (rewriting everything is a huge commitment), it can mean that the original purpose of the curriculum becomes lost and you end up with what Mary Myatt terms "gallimaufry".[2]

I think that, every so often, we need to take a deep breath, grab a piece of blank paper and start from scratch. This gives us the opportunity to stop and think about what we want our curriculum to deliver, the journey we want to take our pupils on. As with many journeys, we want to start with identifying the end point. What do you want your pupils to be able to do by the end of their time with you? If there were no national curriculum and no exams, if nobody were watching, what do you think is important?

For me, in my subject of geography, it is that pupils leave being able to understand why the world is the way it is. I want them to understand why landscapes look the way they do and why places are the way they are. I want them to be able to stand on a mountain and read the landscape as it unfurls before them. I want them to be able to turn on the news and make sense of what they see. This, then, is my curriculum intent.

Once you have articulated the intent of your own curriculum, your programme of study should naturally follow from it. What do pupils need to know, understand and be able to do in order for your intent to be realised? You can start brainstorming topics, texts or historical periods and events to focus in on. Once you have done this, you can look back at any statutory curricula or the demands of the exam board to see if there is anything else you *have* to add. The extent to which you will need to do this will depend on the amount of freedom your subject allows. When I did this, I realised that I wanted my pupils to know much more about the geography of the Middle East and Russia than our current programme of study allowed and that there were topics on the programme that really didn't need to be there.

---

2 Mary Myatt, *The Curriculum: Gallimaufry to Coherence* (Woodbridge: John Catt Educational, 2018).

INTERWEAVING

Another advantage of ripping up your programme of study and starting again is that you can look at the way in which topics are ordered. When these programmes of study grow organically, and new bits and pieces get added and taken away, the original flow of the curriculum (assuming it ever had one) can be lost. If we aren't careful, we find that one topic follows another simply because we are in a new term and something has to happen next.

As Christine Counsell explained in her talk at the 2018 researchEd National Conference in London, we would, ideally, conduct research into the structure of our programmes of study and so have some sort of empirical proof regarding what pupils should study in what order. Unfortunately, no such studies have yet been published, and so we will have to rely on common sense and our own understanding of the subject. Some subjects may lend themselves more naturally to a ready-made structure. For example, a chronological structure is often used in history and in art. For the rest of us, though, we need another way to work out what should be taught when. One way to approach this is to write out the topics on a large piece of paper and draw arrows to show how the learning in one topic supports another. This should reveal which topics need to come first.

For example, when putting together our programme of study, we decided that we wanted our regional study to look at east Africa. To engage with this successfully, pupils needed to have a good understanding of development studies, weather, climate and tectonics (to understand the landscape). Therefore, we knew that the regional study needed to come after these topics.

Another benefit of carrying out this exercise is that it helps you to identify opportunities for interweaving material. Interweaving is the practice of breaking away from the convention of teaching topics to completion in turn and, instead, teaching multiple topics alongside each other. For example, an English class might study *Romeo and Juliet* on Monday, work on their anthology of poems from different cultures on Wednesday, study non-fiction writing techniques on Thursday and return to *Romeo and Juliet* on Friday.

It is thought that this spacing of topics will bring several benefits. Firstly, it gives more opportunity for pupils to start to forget about a topic and then be reminded of it. Retrieval becomes a much more important part of the learning process. If pupils look at a topic over sequential lessons, they can move on to the next lesson much more easily. The learning may *feel* easier, but this easiness may be something of a trap. We need pupils to think hard, and spacing in this way creates what Elizabeth and Robert Bjork call "desirable difficulties".[3]

Interweaving vs interleaving

Interweaving of material in the way I have discussed is, more often than not, erroneously called "interleaving".[4] Interleaving refers to something much more specific – the teaching of very similar material side by side so as to draw out contrasts and make comparison easier. A potential benefit of interleaving is that pupils are better able to make connections between parts of the course and see the differences between things that might otherwise cause confusion. For example, pupils might confuse the art of Constable, Turner and Monet if they simply study each one in turn. If, instead, they studied all three in interleaved lessons then they are more likely to draw out the differences in techniques and approach, and thus discern between them.

For these reasons, both interweaving and interleaving are becoming increasingly popular approaches to curriculum design and, as with anything that is becoming the fashion, the teacher who is teaching like nobody's watching needs to take a long hard look at it and be aware of potential problems. The first thing that you may notice is that school timetables naturally lead to spaced practice of material. Pupils do an hour of one subject, then another, and yet another, and so on. They never really experience the kinds of massed practice that interleaving is designed to work around.

Secondly, few subject teachers see pupils often enough to interleave in the way described in the English example. English and maths teachers may see their classes several times a week and be able to mix in different topics but most non-core

3 Elizabeth L. Bjork and Robert Bjork, Making things hard on yourself, but in a good way: creating desirable difficulties to enhance learning. In Morton A. Gernsbacher, Richard W. Pew, Leaetta M. Hough and James Pomerantz (eds), *Psychology and the Real World: Essays Illustrating Fundamental Contributions to Society*, 2nd edn (New York: Worth Publishers, 2011), pp. 56–64.

4 Mark Enser, Interleaving: are we getting it all wrong?, *TES* (27 February 2019). Available at: https://www.tes.com/news/interleaving-are-we-getting-it-all-wrong.

subjects are lucky to have two lessons with a class in a week. Add in time missed for school photos, trips, INSET days, holidays and all the other calendared events that get in the way of the supposed curriculum model, and pupils may go a week or two without a lesson. This is likely to mean that if you try interleaving in this way, pupils will be waiting weeks to return to a particular topic, meaning material is spaced too far apart for optimal retrieval.

There is a way of working around this problem and still seeing the benefits of spacing - and that is to stick to teaching a topic at a time, but to interweave elements of other topics through it. For example, we start Year 8 with a topic on plate tectonics:

- Pupils study the movement of the earth's plates and the impacts of different types of volcanic eruption. We then leave the topic there.
- However, they return to it in the next topic on east Africa when they look at its landscape and the formation of the Great Rift Valley. At this point, they have to retrieve and revisit what they learnt in the previous unit and also make the connections between these two parts of their schema.
- They then go on to look at their local landscape in East Sussex and the formation of Wealden Anticline (which involves tectonic processes). Again, they revisit the idea of plate movement and connect different parts of their schema.
- In their final topic, they look at Haiti and consider why it is the least economically developed country in the western hemisphere. To consider this question, they look at the tectonic activity in the region and consider the impact that earthquakes have had on the country.

Whilst some of these connections will occur quite naturally throughout your curriculum, it really helps to plan them out in this way and to ensure that key concepts, and particularly threshold concepts (which we'll explore in a moment), are being revisited and interweaved throughout.

FERTILE QUESTIONS

Was Hamlet really mad? Who are the winners and losers in Nigeria's economic growth? Was a second world war inevitable? All of these could be considered as fertile questions.

As we saw in Chapters 2 and 3, input and application are usually best broken up into small chunks. We introduce an idea, explain and demonstrate it, then pupils practise applying it, then we check their understanding and give them feedback. A potential weakness of this approach is that each "chunk" of a topic can end up isolated from the rest and we can lose the sense that we are going somewhere with it. Fertile questions help us to overcome this problem by providing an underpinning big question that all the small chunks are contributing towards.

In *Creating Outstanding Classrooms*, Oliver Knight and David Benson draw on six characteristics of what they call "fertile questions" to help them form the big questions to sit behind a topic. They suggest a good fertile question is:

- An open question.
- An undermining question.
- A rich question.
- A connected question.
- A charged question.
- A practical question.[5]

For this reason, we want to create a fertile question that runs over several lessons, and preferably uses things learnt in previous topics, so that synoptic links are built up. For example, in order to answer, "Who are the winners and losers in Nigeria's economic development?", pupils would first need to learn about:

- What we mean by economic development.

---

5 Oliver Knight and David Benson, *Creating Outstanding Classrooms: A Whole-School Approach* (Abingdon: Routledge, 2014), p. 79.

- How to use development indicators.
- The changing indicators in Nigeria.
- The way in which Nigeria's economy has changed.
- The oil industry and the role of transnational companies such as Shell.
- How urban and rural areas differ.
- Regional variations in development.

Only once they have learnt all of this, in those all-important chunks, can they put it all together to answer their fertile question.

These fertile questions can act as a framing device for parts of your programme of study and be revisited throughout the lesson:

- You can introduce a fertile question at the beginning of a topic and discuss with the class what they will need to learn in order to answer it.
- Then individual tasks within a lesson can be linked back to the fertile question so that they understand where this task is leading.
- The end of the lesson can, in part, be used to reflect on progress towards answering this fertile question.

THRESHOLD CONCEPTS

When putting together a programme of study it can feel as though everything is important. And, indeed, it should be - you wouldn't be wasting everyone's time by teaching it otherwise. But what if some things were more important than others? Things you should really emphasise the teaching of, spend more time on and revisit more often?

These all-important elements of the curriculum are the threshold concepts. The idea of threshold concepts goes back to two economics lecturers, Jan Meyer and Ray Land, who noticed that some students just seemed to get stuck on a course and would stop making progress.[6] They suggested that this was because they hadn't grasped certain key elements of the subject - threshold concepts - without which they couldn't understand what came next.

These threshold concepts could include an understanding of:

- Figurative language in English.
- The role of cells in biology.
- The differences between metals and non-metals in chemistry.
- Sustainability in geography.

Meyer and Land identified certain key classifying features of threshold concepts. They are:

- Transformative: they change the way in which you see the world.
- Troublesome: they might seem counterintuitive or alien.
- Irreversible: the transformative nature means that once they are learnt, the concepts are unlikely to be forgotten.
- Integrated: they reveal connections between the different parts of the discipline.
- Bounded: despite this integration, these concepts only apply within defined parameters.
- Discursive: they lead to the development of new language.[7]

By identifying the threshold concepts in your subject, or within each topic, you can start to plan them into your programme of study. For example, you might want to make sure that they are introduced early on and revisited often. You could also regularly test to check that pupils have understood them, and have plans in place to help those who have not (pre-planned catch-up homework works a treat here - we'll see how in Chapter 6).

6 Jan H. F. Meyer and Ray Land, Threshold concepts and troublesome knowledge: linkages to ways of thinking and practising within the disciplines. In Chris Rust (ed.), *Improving Student Learning: Theory and Practice Ten Years On* (Oxford: Oxford Centre for Staff and Learning Development, 2003), pp. 412–424.

7 Precis quoted from Enser, *Making Every Geography Lesson Count*, p. 23.

KEY POINTS

- Programmes of study develop over time, and, if we aren't careful, their original purpose can be lost.
- Whilst it would be desirable to take each pupil's previous knowledge into account, it might not be possible.
- Interleaving involves the contrasting of two ideas in one lesson. It is unlikely to be a useful mechanism for curriculum design. Interweaving of ideas has more potential.
- We need to be aware of the underpinning threshold concepts in our subject and ensure that pupils are secure on them.
- Fertile questions help to keep the big ideas of our subject front and centre, even as we teach it in smaller chunks.

REFLECTIONS

- When was your curriculum last mapped out from scratch? What has changed since?
- What is the aim of your curriculum? How is this aim enacted?
- Pick one topic. What is the fertile question you hope pupils will be able to answer by the end?
- Which threshold concepts will they have to understand?
- How does this topic link to previous topics?
- When will they return to the ideas in this topic?

CHAPTER 6

THE SUPER-CURRICULUM

The term "super-curriculum", like most educational buzzwords, seems to have appeared in our world fully grown and powerful. I can only assume that there are meetings held somewhere in which a group of shadowy educationalists sit around and decide that terms such as *wave one intervention, tier 2 vocabulary* and, now, *super-curriculum* should be launched into our classrooms, but if this is the case, I'm missing an invitation.

According to James Priory, the super-curriculum:

> represents all those opportunities to develop depth and breadth of learning which extend beyond what the curriculum requires. … It enables pupils to develop specialist knowledge in areas that already seize their interest, but it can also inspire curiosity about areas previously unknown and unventured.[1]

There is a clear overlap between the idea of a super-curriculum and that of extra-curricular activities. Whereas extracurricular activities sit outside the school curriculum, the super-curriculum seeks to build on and extend it. However, as Robin Macpherson points out:

> This is intended to add intellectual value, and provide additional stretch beyond the regular curriculum. The fact that most schools feel the need to provide this – thus

1 James Priory, What is the super curriculum?, *School House* (2018). Available at: https://www.schoolhousemagazine.co.uk/education/what-is-the-super-curriculum/.

demanding a lot of teacher time and effort – says a lot about the limitations of the regular curriculum.[2]

Macpherson suggests that we should avoid a scattergun approach to the super-curriculum, of offering an almost random selection of talks, trips and events - and instead begin by looking at our existing curriculum and asking ourselves what it doesn't cover that we feel is important. As he points out, this can be a way of increasing teacher autonomy and wresting control of the curriculum away from those who impose one on us, be they exam boards, central government or MATs. This is where I think the concept of the super-curriculum meets the remit of this book. It poses the question of how teachers can use the super-curriculum to support what is learnt in class (and so be effective) without increasing demands on their time (and so be efficient). Can we do this in a way that helps us, as teachers, reclaim control of what is taught in our subjects? Can we develop a super-curriculum like nobody's watching?

This chapter attempts to answer these questions. It takes a very loose definition of a super-curriculum as "activities outside the classroom that build on what happens in class". As such, it considers the role of cultural capital, reading lists, homework, field trips and catch-all "super-curricular" activities.

CULTURAL CAPITAL AND POWERFUL KNOWLEDGE

Teaching can feel like a Sisyphean task, especially if pupils lack cultural capital. Those with this capital knock each ball out of the park, whereas those who lack it must feel like salmon struggling to reach their spawning grounds. Waiting for these pupils to grasp your point leaves you feeling like an ice age has been and gone, and as soon as you have helped them understand that point it is time to help them understand the next. You might as well be painting the Forth Bridge.

2 Robin Macpherson, Designing a super-curriculum, *Wellington Learning and Research Centre* [blog] (21 February 2017). Available at: https://learning.wellingtoncollege.org.uk/designing-a-super-curriculum/.

The previous paragraph shows why cultural capital is important. To make sense of it you would need to know all of the following:

- Sisyphus is a character from Greek mythology whose punishment was to push a heavy boulder up a mountain for all of eternity, only to have it roll back down each time he reached the top.
- Knocking the ball out of the park is a reference to baseball and suggests doing something very effectively.
- Salmon swim upstream, against the current, to spawn.
- Ice ages take a long time to pass.
- The Forth Bridge is so long that as soon as it has been painted, it needs doing again from the beginning.

And, of course:

- Cultural capital is that which we have that lets us *fit in* with a social group. This could be mannerisms, a style of dress or an accent (that connote something about our social status), but it also includes what we know, as this lets us converse with others in the group on an equal footing.[3] We understand their allusions.

This final element of cultural capital - what we know - ties into the idea of powerful knowledge. In *Bringing Knowledge Back In,* Michael Young coined the term to describe that knowledge which stands apart from everyday knowledge - it is powerful as it allows us to look beyond the limits of our own experience.[4] This knowledge allows us to join in conversations about the wider world and understand more of what we see and hear.

We also need to consider a third overlapping concept: that of cultural literacy. This idea, developed by E. D. Hirsch, Jr., suggests that there is a body of knowledge that people need to have in order to make sense of contemporary society.[5] Without this

---

3 Pierre Bourdieu, Cultural reproduction and social reproduction. In Richard Brown (ed.), *Knowledge, Education and Cultural Change* (Abingdon: Routledge, 2018 [1973]), pp. 71-112.

4 Michael Young, *Bringing Knowledge Back In: From Social Constructivism to Social Realism in the Sociology of Education* (Abingdon: Routledge, 2007).

5 Eric Donald Hirsch, Jr., *Cultural Literacy: What Every American Needs to Know* (Boston, MA: Houghton Mifflin, 1987).

literacy, we might struggle to read the front page of a daily newspaper. Not because we couldn't read the individual words but because we couldn't understand it in context.

Cultural literacy has strong implications for how well we can recall what we have read. In one experiment, researchers asked participants to read an article about a baseball game. Those who already had a good knowledge of the game were able to recall much more about it, and more accurately, than those who did not. Problems with comprehending a text could have as much to do with cultural literacy as with the ability to decode individual words.[6] It could therefore be argued that the best remedy for poor literacy isn't more practice of generic "reading skills" but instead to direct effort at becoming more knowledgeable and so better able to make sense of the words you are seeing.

This, then, is an area we might want to focus on when considering our super-curriculum. How could we design activities outside of the classroom to improve a pupil's cultural capital, cultural literacy and powerful knowledge? Our time in the classroom is very limited, and it is further limited by constantly filling in gaps in pupils' underdeveloped knowledge. The more we can do to help pupils learn more about the wider world, the easier our job in the classroom becomes. As ever, it comes down to finding effective and efficient ways to do this.

HOMEWORK

There are many divisive topics in education, and homework is right up there amongst them. There will be few teachers who won't have sat through parents' evenings and been told that they give too much homework by some parents and too little by others. On top of concerns from parents, homework is also often monitored by the SLT, with timetables that should be adhered to and certain kinds of tasks preferred or frowned upon depending on the prevailing mood.

6 For more on this see Daniel Willingham, School time, knowledge, and reading comprehension, *Daniel Willingham - Science and Education* [blog] (7 March 2012). Available at: http://www.danielwillingham.com/daniel-willingham-science-and-education-blog/school-time-knowledge-and-reading-comprehension.

This pressure to set homework just because the timetable says it should be set, and to set that type of homework just because it is the flavour of the month, creates a host of problems. It means that it is often an afterthought, rather than intrinsic to the lesson, or involves setting tasks that achieve very little in terms of what pupils have learnt from the process.

One problem is that homework is completed without the input of an expert in the subject (you, the teacher). As we saw in Part I, input is a vital part of the learning process. If homework tasks are based on the input pupils received in class then this might mitigate against some of the problems (although even when pupils are applying what they have learnt, ongoing monitoring helps[7]), but in many schools there is a preference for project-type work that is only tangentially linked to what is studied in class.

Whilst this might make sense in terms of increasing a pupil's cultural capital and cultural literacy beyond what is offered by the curriculum, it also presents problems. One issue is that without guidance, pupils simply learn and embed misconceptions. I remember one occasion after my pupils were asked to produce a report on London, when I received a number of pieces in which they had mixed up information about London, UK, and London, Canada. On another occasion, pupils completed work on climate change in which many of them had discussed, at length, how global warming was caused by a hole in the ozone layer.

Other homework projects can create a large amount of work with very little learning. Building model volcanoes may sound like a good idea, but pupils end up knowing no more about volcanoes than they did when they started. Nevertheless, these types of homework projects have been very popular in some schools, and teachers have been directed to create and set them.

Of course, if we teach like nobody's watching, we don't need to worry about such shifts in what outside observers would like to see in our classrooms, and outside them. We can set homework to support what pupils are learning in class and help them go beyond it. This might include:

- **Finishing classwork.** This has been very unpopular at times but makes a lot of sense. Once pupils have had high-quality instruction, and had the start of their

7 Rosenshine, Principles of instruction.

application monitored, they may need little more guidance from you. It makes perfect sense, therefore, for this work to be started in class and then completed at home. Checking and discussing this work at the start of the following lesson is also a natural way to review previous learning.

- **Pre-reading.** Similar to finishing off classwork, you might decide that if a lesson requires pupils to read through resources, then this is best done at home. They could read it through, answer some comprehension questions or write a summary: something to ensure that they are actually having to think about the material. You would still need to consider whether pupils might have picked up any misconceptions from their unguided reading that would need exploring in the subsequent lesson.
- **Revision.** If we aren't careful, revision can be seen as something that happens just before an exam. As we discussed in Chapter 1, however, it is important that revision is an ongoing part of the learning process. We can use homework time for this by setting work that's not about the current topic but previous ones. This has the benefit that pupils are unlikely to pick up misconceptions as they should already be familiar with the ideas. It also means that they have the chance to review things they have looked at in the past but in the context of a different topic. They may see it in a new light and so develop their schema. For example, when studying *A Christmas Carol* in class, you might set homework based on their work last term on *An Inspector Calls* that asks them to look at issues of class and injustice. They may start to see parallels between the Birlings and Scrooge that deepen their understanding of both.
- **Extension.** This final suggestion probably has more to do with developing a super-curriculum in the purest sense than the other three do. There are some things that we know would be useful or important for pupils to know but that we just can't find time for in the in-school curriculum. For example, we touch on the rise of Islamist militants in north and west Africa in our curriculum when we look at its impact on tourism in Tunisia and on internal migration in Nigeria. Pupils know enough about it to make sense of the issue but would certainly benefit from a deeper understanding. Homework could be used to explore this in more depth by issuing pupils with texts to read, documentaries to watch and questions to answer.

However we decide to use homework, we need to consider that pupils will be doing it with minimal guidance and that we must prepare to compensate for any problems caused. Instructions need to be crystal clear and pupils need to have a very good understanding of the topic before they begin. If we ensure this, we can reclaim homework as something that everyone genuinely benefits from rather than something set to balance the competing demands imposed upon us.

READING LISTS

One way in which some schools develop their super-curriculum is by providing pupils with reading lists in each subject, in the style of those given to undergraduate students. The rationale behind this is easy to understand: we know that there is a clear link between how much pupils read and their attainment.[8] We want pupils to increase their cultural literacy and one way to do this is to increase the amount of high-quality reading they do. We want to expose them to ideas that they might not come across in their everyday life, or in books they regularly read, and reading lists are one way to increase this exposure.

There are issues, however. As we saw at the start of this chapter, Robin Macpherson alluded to the risk of creating a scattergun approach to the super-curriculum. Some pupils *might* read something from the list, others *might* read something else. It is going to be very difficult to tie what they are reading from these lists into what is happening in the classroom. Therefore, the curriculum isn't really being extended: something new is being added for some pupils.

Of course, another issue is that many pupils (I'll go out on a limb here and say most) will simply ignore the list. We could find that we have spent hours curating a list of excellent resources that will simply gather dust. The few pupils who chose to read books from the list are more likely to be those who already have well-developed cultural literacy. Part of the issue here will be with access. Where will pupils be getting these books and articles from? Does your school library stock them in sufficient quantity? Are they available for free online, and do pupils have internet access?

8 Christina Clark and Jonathan Douglas, *Young People's Reading and Writing: An In-Depth Study Focusing on Enjoyment, Behaviour, Attitudes and Attainment* (London: National Literacy Trust, 2011). Available at: https://files.eric.ed.gov/fulltext/ED521656.pdf.

These problems need not be insurmountable. Firstly, we want to make it as easy as possible for pupils to access high-quality reading. My department has a bookcase full of such books that pupils are free to borrow. Having these to hand also makes it easier to make recommendations following conversations with pupils. Personal recommendations carry more weight than a list given to every pupil. We source these books largely from our own collections and accept that it is always possible that a book might not come back. We also solicit donations from parents and people in the local community.

We can make reading more accessible by sourcing as much as we can online. One way to achieve this is to start a blog where you can compile articles and news stories on particular topics. This means that if a pupil wants to read up on river flooding, the Battle of Britain or genetic research, it is quick and easy for them to find what they need. As well as sharing the link, you can provide a brief explanation of the text and any unfamiliar terms to make it more accessible (think about the example of the need for cultural capital earlier in this chapter).

As well as making the reading available, we also need to incentivise as many pupils as possible to make use of it. If your school already has a popular rewards system then it should be possible to take advantage of that and reward pupils for answering comprehension questions on reading topics. You could also try tapping into your pupils' competitive nature with a readers' league table, awarding points based on the complexity of what is read. The aim, of course, is to get to a point where you don't need such incentives for pupils to read quality material about your subject, but this is probably going to involve a long, slow change in culture.

Finally, we want to make sure that we avoid that scattergun approach and tie what pupils are reading into the in-school curriculum. We could achieve this by moving from a general reading list to something more bespoke for each topic, asking pupils to read a particular book or, more practically, a series of shorter articles. This would support what they are learning in class but have the advantage of going further than we have time for and bringing in a wider range of ideas and perspectives. Reading these articles might be a better use of homework time than many other tasks, and has the additional benefit of reducing marking!

FIELD TRIPS

As a geography teacher, I feel naturally predisposed to see field trips as a good thing. Like anything else which passes as an unquestioned positive in education, we need to look very carefully to see whether it really is. Some field trips clearly have value if they allow pupils to do things they couldn't do in the classroom. If we want pupils to know how to carry out a geographical investigation, we need them to practise carrying one out. Other field trips offer pupils experiences that we feel are important on a deeper level, such as visiting Auschwitz or carrying out charity work in another country. These experiences open up our pupils' eyes to a world beyond the everyday and are another way of creating powerful knowledge.

However, field trips are not without their problems, which, of course, need careful consideration. Firstly, there is an issue of cost. A trip into the nearby town centre to do some field work may cost very little and therefore be open to everyone, but what about a trip to Iceland to see volcanoes first-hand? How many pupils will be able to afford to come on this trip? Do we run the risk of creating a two-tier education system within a school, in which some pupils have access to a super-curriculum and others don't? It is likely that many of those pupils who can afford to go on these kinds of trips are the ones who least need the opportunity to go.

Secondly, we need to look at what these trips are actually offering. As ever, we should be asking the question that sits at the heart of this book: would we do this if nobody was watching? If there was no external pressure to run it, would it still go ahead? We may want to ask:

- Are the trips in place because they look good in the school prospectus or because they are developing our pupils' understanding of the world around them?
- Do the pupils you are taking on a ski trip already go skiing with their families?
- Are the pupils getting off the plane from Iceland about to jet off to Tenerife?
- What are pupils experiencing when they go to that theme park that you think adds value to their education?

If we are not careful, we spend our time becoming travel agents rather than teachers.

This leads us to our third consideration when planning field trips as part of a super-curriculum: the opportunity cost. This is a term often used in economics to show that we need to take into account the benefit we didn't accrue whilst pursuing another course of action. Planning trips can take up a vast amount of time. Even a reasonably simple trip like going to a national park will involve booking coaches, sorting out parking permits, collecting equipment, preparing resources, writing permission letters, chasing permission slips and payment, checking medical details, creating a risk assessment, preparing activities for the day, sorting staffing, briefing the staff and setting cover work. All before you have left the building.

At the very least, we need to consider the time it has taken to do all of this and then consider what we could have done instead. Was this trip worth the scheme of work that was never written? The staff training that was never prepared? The detailed mock exam analysis and feedback that was left on the backburner? If your answer is "Yes, it is worth it", then excellent, it sounds like a trip that should go ahead. But it is worth having this conversation first.

KEY POINTS

- A super-curriculum shouldn't be a random collection of extra activities on offer to pupils, but a carefully curated extension of the taught curriculum.
- Pupils with greater cultural literacy are usually able to comprehend texts better than those without it. Widening what a pupil knows will help in a range of subjects.
- Homework tasks can create an unsustainable workload for both teachers and pupils, and lead to very little gain for either. Like everything else, homework should be effective and efficient and not done to placate outside observers.
- Field trips and field work are not the same thing. We need to give field trips careful consideration to establish exactly who is going to benefit from it and what the cost is.
- If we want pupils to read about our subject, we need to do more than provide a reading list.

REFLECTIONS

- How culturally literate are your pupils? Would they be able to make sense of newspaper editorial?
- What activities do you, your department or your school offer outside the taught curriculum? Is there a reason why this isn't covered in class time?
- Which books are you currently reading that link to your subject? Is there some way to build extracts of these into your lessons?
- What homework do you set? What are you trying to achieve? Is it working?

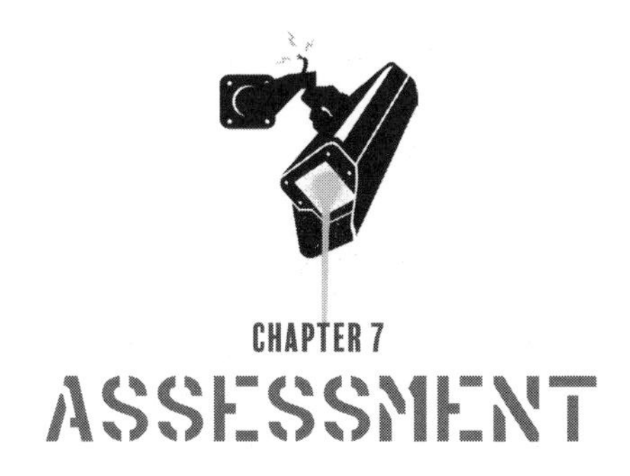

CHAPTER 7

ASSESSMENT

Alongside marking, and closely related to it, nothing fills a teacher's time quite like assessment. The increased workload created by assessment has been amplified by the accountability culture, which has led to some school leaders desiring to know exactly how pupils are progressing at all times. This, in turn, has meant that assessment has come to mean teachers reporting on whether pupils are on track towards their attainment targets. This is problematic for a number of reasons.

The problem of reporting

The first problem is that assessment has become tied to reporting to different audiences. We want to pass the results on to the pupils, the parents and school leaders, but the information that each group wants - and can make use of - is likely to be very different. Therefore, the form of the assessment gets determined by the need to report on the outcome. The needs of the teacher in all of this can easily be overlooked.

The problem with "on track"

The second problem is with trying to determine whether a pupil is "on track". In secondary schools, this usually refers to being on track to reach their GCSE target grade. These targets are based on their Key Stage 2 results, so, theoretically at least, we can create their GCSE target the second they walk through our doors in Year 7. It is understandable that we would desire to know who is on track for these targets throughout the year, and over the five years they are with us. If we knew that a pupil was not on track, we could intervene earlier to support them. We could give better advice about what they will be able to do post-16, depending on whether they hit those targets or not. But just because this is desirable doesn't mean it is possible. How a pupil does on one assessment tells me very little about how they will perform on another one in years to come. Too much will change in the meantime.[1]

The problem with current attainment

The third problem is that not only can we not really say whether pupils are "on track" towards a target grade, we can't really say where their current attainment is with any accuracy either. A statement about current attainment is summative and, as such, we need a common understanding about what it means. If I say a pupil is currently at a B in geography, the criteria for this B needs to mean the same thing to me as it does to you, and to the exam board.

The problem with applying GCSE grades to assessments is that the criteria will be different to that used in the final exam. It is unlikely that any in-class assessment will be on the whole of the GCSE domain, so pupils have less to revise and will need to demonstrate less knowledge. Pupils may be better prepared for mid-year assessments and have a better idea of what will be on the paper. On top of this, grade boundaries shift year on year to take account of differences in the difficulty of the paper. What are the chances that the bit of the paper you are using for an assessment has the same level of difficulty as the final exam on which published boundaries are based?

The problems with reporting to different audiences, the impossibility of knowing whether a pupil is "on track" and the lack of a shared meaning when we attach GCSE grades to assessment outcomes mean that many school assessment, tracking and reporting systems are producing nothing but junk data which teachers are then expected to respond to and use to inform decisions. How might assessment be different if we left it up to the teacher? How do we assess like nobody's watching?

1 See Mike Treadaway, Why measuring pupil progress involves more than taking a straight line, *FFT Education Datalab* [blog] (5 March 2015). Available at: https://ffteducationdatalab.org.uk/2015/03/why-measuring-pupil-progress-involves-more-than-taking-a-straight-line/.

WHY DO TEACHERS ASSESS?

Teachers assess pupils for a very simple reason. We want to know if they have learnt what we want them to learn. Graham Nuthall's *The Hidden Lives of Learners* makes it clear that learning is an invisible process, and that teachers often have misconceptions about what pupils have actually come away with after a lesson.[2] Assessment is designed to make this learning visible to the teacher so that we can respond to any gaps and adjust our teaching in the future.

This simplifying of assessment goals has led to the suggestion that we should see the curriculum as the assessment model. In other words, we can define progress as pupils learning what we intend them to learn. We don't need to try to turn this into a summative grade or level: they have either learnt what we thought they should or they haven't. If they haven't, we can then take action to address this. We can even do this with domain skills. For example, what skills are involved in writing a good analytical essay? Break the task up into its component parts and see if the pupil can or cannot do these things.

Objectively assessing what has been learnt also allows us to make judgements about how effective a particular lesson or strategy has been. One of the reasons why the kinds of fads that I mentioned in the introduction were able to linger is that as a profession we weren't good enough at evaluating whether an approach was really working.

It can be tempting to try to see whether a lesson has been effective by looking at what is happening in the classroom. If pupils are quiet and getting on with their work, it feels like learning is happening. If they are completing a lot of work, if this work looks correct, if some of them can answer the questions you pose, it looks like learning is happening. Professor Robert Coe has identified a number of these so-called poor proxies for learning that are often used in schools to judge whether teaching has been effective.[3] These include:

- Pupils being busy and producing a lot of work.

2 Nuthall, *The Hidden Lives of Learners*.

3 Robert Coe, Improving Education: A Triumph of Hope over Experience, Inaugural Lecture of Professor Robert Coe, Durham University (18 June 2013), p. 12. Available at: http://www.cem.org/attachments/publications/ImprovingEducation2013.pdf.

- Pupils seeming interested in the topic.
- Pupils receiving a lot of feedback.
- A calm classroom.
- The curriculum is being covered.
- At least some pupils have supplied correct answers.

The problem with these proxies is that they can be evident even when no learning is taking place. A history class might be calm and quiet when they are just colouring in a picture of Henry VIII. There might be a lot of work being done in a geography class, but the tasks are too easy and require little thought. The curriculum might be being covered in science, but perhaps the pupils aren't paying close enough attention and the content isn't being retained. This is why teachers turn to assessments rather than exercise books to find out if pupils have learnt what they should have. With a well-planned assessment (we'll define what this looks like in just a moment) you can strip everything else away and just focus on knowledge retention.

HOW DO PUPILS BENEFIT FROM ASSESSMENT?

It is not only teachers who benefit from meaningful assessment; pupils do too. Firstly, because their teacher can then respond to the assessment results and so improve their teaching in the future, and, secondly, because they benefit from a positive washback, what Henry Roediger et al. call "indirect effects of testing" - benefits that occur as a side effect of the assessment process.[4]

- Pupils benefit from retrieval practice as they would from any test or quiz. They are being asked to recall what they have learnt (see Chapter 1).
- They have the opportunity to identify gaps in their own learning and so seek to address them.

4 Henry L. Roediger, III, Adam L. Putnam and Megan A. Smith, Ten benefits of testing and their applications to educational practice. In Jose P. Mestre and Brian H. Ross (eds), *The Psychology of Learning and Motivation. Vol. 55: Cognition in Education* (San Diego, CA: Elsevier Academic Press, 2011), pp. 1-36 at p. 2.

- They know that they have an assessment to prepare for, so it encourages them to focus.
- Pupils are prompted to better organise their knowledge during the revision process. They review what they have learnt and, in doing so, restructure it. Their schema develops.
- The assessment process can help with metacognition as pupils have to think about their own learning.
- It improves the transfer of knowledge to new scenarios.
- It gives feedback to their teachers.
- It encourages them to study, which means they are spending longer learning about whatever it is that we have deemed important enough to assess.

It is entirely possible that a culture of high-stakes testing creates problems for our young people, but within this debate we don't want to lose sight of the fact that testing also has its advantages. We want to find ways of keeping the advantages whilst avoiding the stress of high-stakes accountability. This comes down to well-designed and well-used assessment.

PRINCIPLES OF ASSESSMENT DESIGN

Effective assessment design is a complex business and the fact that teachers are asked to create assessments with very little understanding of the underlying principles strikes me as madness. It seems to suggest that despite much stock being placed in the outcome of assessments - seen in ever more esoteric tracking systems - much less thought is given to how these outcomes are produced. This is a huge mistake. Putting junk data into a tracking system means that junk data comes out. So why is so much of the assessment data generated in schools junk? Let's explore.

What are we assessing?

The first question that we need to ask when designing an assessment is about what it is we actually want to assess. This is the *construct*. It is important to remember that an assessment can never ask questions about everything that has been covered in the curriculum. Even if we assess regularly throughout the year, we will have to confine ourselves to a sample part of the curriculum. We therefore have to make a careful judgement about which parts we want to include and whether these are representative of the rest. This is why assessment needs to be tied to the intent of the curriculum.

If I have decided that the aim of a unit is for pupils to understand how rivers shape the land, then I need to select questions that assess this understanding. I won't be able to ask them about every form of erosion or transportation, or every landform or flood event, but I will need to select from within these areas to make a valid judgement about whether they have the understanding that I am looking for. I can ask questions that require them to apply their understanding to particular examples: What will happen to the meander pictured over time? Why might a waterfall have formed on the stretch of the river shown on the map?

Another thing to consider is the balance between the substantive and disciplinary knowledge that we are assessing. Substantive knowledge is the "stuff" we expect our pupils to remember about the topic we have taught and is generally easier to assess. Do they know what photosynthesis is? Can they explain how Orwell's choice of language creates a sense of tension at the start of *1984*? Just what will happen to that meander? All of this is substantive knowledge.

Disciplinary knowledge can be trickier to pin down. It is the knowledge of how the subject works and of how we create new knowledge in that discipline. For example, what are the stages of a geographical enquiry? How should historians approach their sources? What is the significance of the scientific method? These are important parts of the curriculum but can be overlooked in assessment design until we reach formal assessments at the end of the key stage. When creating our own assessments, we need to consider how to include disciplinary knowledge.

If you aren't crystal clear about the intended outcomes of your curriculum then you will always struggle to assess progress within it. Without this focus, you are left looking for generic aspects of your subject to assess – such as whether pupils can explain their answer or use examples - but will not be able to assess the learning that has taken place and so miss out on the real advantages of assessment. The assessment becomes uncoupled from the curriculum.

How do we make valid judgements?

If we can agree that what we assess is the curriculum, we are still left with the thorny problem of how we make *valid* judgements about whether pupils have learnt the curriculum. Jo-Anne Baird et al. suggest that we should ask ourselves whether the information we gather from an assessment supports the claim we make.[5] In other words, can I use the result of the assessment to say, "Pupil X is Y good at this subject?" It is important to remember that when we talk about validity, we are not talking about the test itself being valid, but rather our judgement or inference based on this test.

The Assessment Lead Programme from Evidence Based Education gives the example of four questions we should ask about the validity of our inference:[6]

1. Face Validity - Is this testing what we want to know?
2. Content Validity - Does this cover everything we want to test?
3. Convergent Validity - Do two tests on the same topic produce the same results?
4. Divergent Validity - Do tests of different things produce different results?

If the same pupil sat two different assessments about rivers, they should do just as well, or badly, on both of them. If they achieve very different results, then it would indicate a weakness in the validity of the inference you can make. Do they understand how rivers shape the land or not? Conversely, if assessments on very different topics, and in different subjects, always produce identical results you may need to consider whether the assessment is only testing very generic skills, rather than specifics about the topic or subject. As Robert Coe says, "The point is not that all assessment has to surprise you, just that in principle surprise has to be possible".[7]

5 Jo-Anne Baird, David Andrich, Therese Hopfenbeck and Gordon Stobart, Assessment and learning: fields apart?, *Assessment in Education: Principles, Policy and Practice* 24(3) (2017): 317-350.

6 See https://evidencebased.education/assessment-academy-assessment-lead-programme/.

7 Robert Coe, But that is NOT AN ASSESSMENT, *CEMblog* [blog] (20 June 2018). Available at: http://www.cem.org/blog/but-that-is-not-an-assessment/.

We also need to consider whether we are actually assessing what we think we are. This problem is often evident when we look at issues of literacy. For example, in my assessment on rivers I might include a passage about the Cumbrian floods and ask pupils questions about the physical and human causes. If a pupil does badly on this question, I might infer that they do not understand these causes, but actually the issue could be that they were not able to comprehend the text. Problems can also arise if we expect pupils to know things that weren't directly taught as part of the curriculum - things we might consider to be "general knowledge". We need to remember that if we expect pupils to know something in an assessment, that is what we are assessing and therefore that is what we are making a judgement about.

How do we assess?

Even once we have created an assessment to interrogate what we think pupils should have learnt and written it in a way that should allow us to make valid inferences, there is still a risk that our inferences may be invalid. The problem is with the way in which the assessments are carried out. Formal summative assessments are carried out in very tightly controlled conditions. Teachers don't know what will be on the paper and neither do the pupils. They work in silence and without access to notes. As far as possible, everything is stripped away other than that which is in their heads.

Contrast this with assessments carried out in schools. Sometimes pupils are told in advance what they will be assessed on, especially if it will be in the form of an essay or report. They may have the opportunity to prepare for this specific assessment title and even to bring notes with them. In this case, we can't make a judgement about how well they have learnt what we want them to have learnt, unless it is all contained within this one assessment title. Even then, we may just be assessing the quality of the notes they brought with them. In these kinds of open book assessments, we need to remember that we cannot make inferences about what the pupils have learnt in terms of the subject content; rather, we can see how they can manipulate that information in the written task.

Even if the pupils don't know what the content of the assessment will be, in most cases their teacher will. Sometimes the teacher will have written the assessment, other times they might have seen it in a shared drive along with the scheme of work or be familiar with it because the same assessment is used year after year. In any case, there is a natural, and possibly even subconscious, desire to teach what is on the test. This again means that we can't make a wider judgement about what pupils have learnt about the whole curriculum, only what they have learnt about the narrow part of the curriculum for which they have been prepared.

If we want to be able to compare how pupils performed against others in their cohort then it is very important that assessments are carried out in the same conditions. If one teacher allows their class to talk or use notes during an assessment, you can't then compare the results with those who didn't. This is often a problem with the so-called "standardised tests" that seem to be popular.[8] The aim to is get a better picture of how your pupils are doing against a national benchmark, which is a desirable aim. But unless everyone is carrying out the tests in identical conditions, with the same level of importance placed on them by the pupils, they are not truly standardised tests and are thus producing junk data.

A final point to consider is that formal, external summative assessments - such as GCSEs and SATs - are marked in a very different way to most internal assessments. External assessments tend to be marked blind, with the examiner having no idea who produced the answer. As a result, they approach the work with fewer preconceived ideas about what the pupil can achieve and bring fewer biases to bear (although handwriting bias is still a significant barrier[9]). A solution would be for teachers within a department to mix up the papers and replace pupils' names with their exam candidate numbers. This would also help to mitigate against variations in marking accuracy.

Reporting the judgement

The final hurdle to overcome in creating a meaningful assessment regards how the data generated is then used. Let's say you've created an assessment that checks what pupils have learnt about a modest representation of the curriculum, made sure that the questions were worded in a way that didn't test general knowledge and checked that everyone was doing the assessment in the same way, and a pupil gets 68%. What now?

8 Becky Allen, What if we cannot measure pupil progress? *Becky Allen* [blog] (23 May 2018). Available at: https://rebeccaallen.co.uk/2018/05/23/what-if-we-cannot-measure-pupil-progress/.

9 Daisy Christodoulou, Could handwriting bias write off exam chances?, *TES* (23 October 2018) Available at: https://www.tes.com/news/could-handwriting-bias-write-exam-chances.

That 68% on its own tells you very little. You could report that they achieved 68%, but is this good? Does it represent "progress"? Consider the following:

- How does that 68% compare with their last assessment? It could be tempting to say that if they got a lower score on their previous assessment then 68% is evidence of progress, but this assumes that the two assessments were of equal difficulty and that they were assessing the exact same part of the curriculum.
- What grade does 68% represent? We could try to apply GCSE grade boundaries to the score. This would be useful as these grades have a shared meaning. It would also be useful as it would give us an indication of whether the pupil is on track towards a target. However, this would only work if your assessment was of an identical difficulty to the paper on which the grade boundaries were based and was completed in identical conditions. If this is not the case, then the grade you ascribe to the score is simply a lie.
- You could report whether you think 68% indicates that the pupil is on track for their target grade. Does this 68% suggest that they are where you'd expect them to be? The problem here is that you would need to know how pupils who achieved 68% in this assessment went on to achieve and, even then, it would only work if there was a consistent pattern. There would almost certainly be too many confounding factors for this to work.

Here we are once again facing the problems highlighted at the start of this chapter. Our desire to know if a pupil is on track - and what their current attainment score is if converted to a GCSE grade - is leading us to attempt the impossible and, in doing so, create meaningless and misleading data. Luckily, there may be an alternative: rank order assessment.

RANK ORDER ASSESSMENT

Rank order assessment strips away most of the problems with progress towards target grades and grade boundaries and instead deals in what we actually know:

- How did that pupil do on that assessment?
- How did that result compare to how others have done?

- Compared to others taking the test, have they done as well as we would expect?

I would suggest that this is how most teachers think about assessment data. They look at the score a pupil gets and compare it to the scores that other pupils got. Rank order assessment just allows us to turn it into a form that might mean more to other people with an interest in how the pupil is doing.

Let's return to the pupil who achieved 68% on their assessment. We have already discussed why we can't turn that into a grade or compare the raw score to a previous assessment, but we can see how they compare with the rest of the class. We could say that they achieved 68%, but the cohort mean was 80%. Now that we have some context, we know that 68% is not an especially strong score. We could also say where they ranked. Perhaps 68% is enough to put them at 125/200. That too provides some context.

What it doesn't do is tell us whether we should be happy with that result for that particular pupil. Is ranking 125/200 where we would expect them to be? What we can do next is compare their rank on this assessment with those on previous assessments. Have they experienced a sudden drop that might be a cause for concern? We could also compare their rank with where we would expect them to be based on the Key Stage 2 data on which their GCSE target is ultimately based. If this pupil ranks 125/200 but they are expected to get some of the highest results in the school, this may be a sign that support is needed. Or that the school needs to consider how realistic their target is.

There are justified concerns about this method of rank order assessment and these usually come down to how this information is communicated to pupils and parents. If a pupil is constantly told they are ranking near the bottom of their cohort, it would seem intuitively true that they will become demotivated and perform even worse in the future. However, researcher Becky Allen's piece on assessment and reporting cites two examples of studies showing that pupil performance improved after some form of public ranking was introduced.[10]

However, even if we are worried about *reporting* rank, it doesn't mean this method can't be used by us in school to work out how pupils are doing. We can decouple

10 Becky Allen, Writing the rules of the grading game (part I): the grade changes the child, *Becky Allen* [blog] (24 April 2019). Available at: https://rebeccaallen.co.uk/2019/04/24/grading-game-part-i/.

the data tracking from the reporting system. And we are of course free, as teachers, to use rank order assessment ourselves to inform our responses to assessment, even if it's not part of our school policy. We don't need to wait for permission when we teach like nobody's watching.

By using rank order assessment we have moved beyond the wishful thinking of the desirable into the realm of what is possible. We are sticking with what we actually know and what will be useful in the classroom. Because, of course, however good our assessment and inference are, what really matters is what we then do with the information.[11]

RESPONDING TO ASSESSMENT

Once we have excellent assessments that allow us to make valid inferences, we can start to think about what we can do with the information. One thing we can't really do is use it formatively. We know how pupils did compared to others (a normative judgement - such as those reached in the reformed GCSEs, in which pupils are scored in relation to others in the cohort) and how they did compared to their previous performance (what is known as an ipsative judgement) but not why. It is entirely possible that they scored badly because they didn't know enough to answer a question, but it could also be that they misread or misunderstood the question, ran out of time, or thought that the answer they gave was *also* right. We won't know which is the case simply by looking at their assessment, and this is why ongoing formative assessment and feedback needs to be an intrinsic part of every lesson and not something saved for assessments (as we discussed in Chapter 4).

DIRT was intended as a way of incorporating formative assessment and feedback in each lesson but has proven to be problematic in practice. It was imposed on teachers with very little thought about the intentions behind it. It became yet another thing we had to demonstrate that we were doing. It turned into something to be put on lesson plans and checklists, and even started to appear in classroom DIRT displays. As such, it is pretty antithetical to those who are teaching like nobody's watching.

11 For a case study on how rank order assessment can be used, see Part III.

DIRT typically involves improving a piece of work, often after an assessment. The pupil completes something, they receive feedback on how to do it better and then make some corrections. This is fine if our objective is for them to eventually be able to produce one really good piece of work which is free from errors. But it may not help in other tasks. It confines feedback to one section of the lesson: "Improve this piece of work you did last week. Now put it to one side and we will move on."

This sends completely the wrong message. Feedback should seek to improve the pupil, not the work. The feedback they receive, however they receive it, should influence the rest of the work they go on to do throughout the lesson and beyond. We want pupils to be thinking about this feedback whenever it is useful, not just at the beginning of a lesson because someone in the SLT has decided it is a "non-negotiable".

Feedback is an integral part of teaching and learning. When we see how a class is doing, and become aware of mistakes and misconceptions, we adjust our teaching and plan to address any shortcomings. We give pupils feedback constantly throughout a lesson. We tell them that a verbal answer is good, then explain that they need to add more detail. We glance at books and remind them that they have just made the same mistake that they made last week. We stop the class to address a point that many seem to be confused on. All of this is about improvement and reflection.

It is important that pupils review their work (it is Barak Rosenshine's final principle of instruction, after all), but this process is too important to be confined to the rushed beginning of a lesson. Instead it needs to be, as it always has been in good classrooms, an ongoing part of the learning process. Pupils should be challenged to read back over and improve their work all the time: at the start of a lesson, in the middle or at the end. None of these occasions needs to be designated DIRT. It is just teaching.

Our ability to respond to a summative assessment is only ever going to be as good as the validity and reliability of the inference we can make from it. If we can make a secure judgement about which pupils are falling behind their peers, we can - at the very least - identify who needs further support. We can sit down with those pupils to look through their assessments and identify the errors they made, then set them practice tasks to help them correct those precise errors. We can also give these pupils more attention in class, if needs be, and use more formative assessment strategies to ensure that the problems are being addressed. This could include quick quizzes or tasks which focus on the exact issues that have been diagnosed. If a pupil was unable to show that they understood the relationship between Macbeth and Lady Macbeth, can they, after some support and additional help, now point to two or three quotes that best sum up their relationship? If a pupil was unable to explain the role of light in plant growth, after some support, can they now explain why so few plants are able to grow on the rainforest floor? As ever, we want to keep it simple.

All this, however, will only be effective if we have identified the right pupils in the first place. Few things are quite as soul destroying for a teacher as running meaningless assessments to generate meaningless data to identify pupils for meaningless interventions.

KEY POINTS

- Many problems in assessment stem from trying to do the impossible just because the impossible is desirable.
- To reach a summative judgement on how well a pupil has achieved, we have to have a shared understanding of what that judgement means.
- To use grade boundaries to inform our judgement, we would have to have pupils complete the same paper in the same conditions.
- We can work around some of the problems with assessment by accepting the limitations of what we can know. We can tell how well a pupil can respond to the questions we ask and how this compares to others who have done the same test.
- Once pupils complete an assessment, we need to respond.
- Formative assessments can be used more diagnostically than summative assessments can, as they should be designed to inform the teacher about exactly what a pupil can or cannot do, or does or does not understand.

REFLECTIONS

- If asked, could you confidently place the pupils in your class in order of highest to lowest current achieving in your subject? If not, is your assessment system working?
- What judgements do you make about the progress your pupils are making? Are these judgements valid?
- As a teacher, what do you need to know about what your pupils have learnt?
- What will you do with this information?

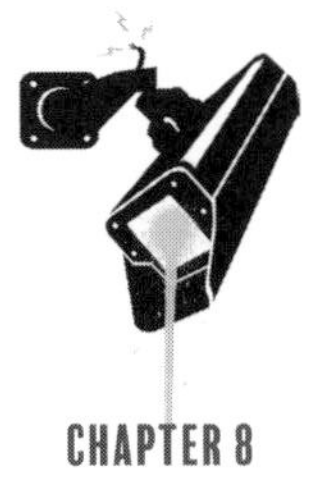

CHAPTER 8

THE DEPARTMENT MEETING

As I have been arguing throughout this book, if we are to teach like nobody's watching, we need to take control of our professional practice. One area in which we can find a surprising amount of freedom is in the time set aside for department meetings. This time, set aside on the calendar in the form of after-school meetings and INSET sessions, is usually under the control of the head of department and is theirs to do with as they see fit. Members of the SLT may try to interject with things that they would like to place on the agenda, but these are easily dealt with (as we shall soon see) and a surprising amount can be achieved in the time we have.

Many problems that we see in schools come from a desire, or at least a requirement, to please a range of people far from the classroom. In a department meeting, we find a smaller group of people with a much better idea of the needs of their pupils in their subject. Our teaching can become much more effective and efficient when we work with a small group of like-minded professionals. For this reason, I think it makes sense to rethink department meetings as department CPD.

In recent years there has been an increasing awareness that generic pedagogy can only take us so far. Every subject is structured, and so should be taught, in a different way. As such, there has been a move away from CPD being delivered to the whole school and towards handing CPD time over to departments, with heads of department delivering it. In terms of school improvement, this makes a lot of sense. Work by Coe et al. found that the evidence about what makes great teaching pointed to strong subject knowledge and an understanding of how the subject worked as the most important factors.[1] This was followed by the quality of

1 Coe et al., *What Makes Great Teaching?*

instruction, which obviously must be supported by excellent subject knowledge to be effective.

It is not only the head of that department who should have control over this time. A good head of department will always welcome ideas from the team about how to make good use of department time and, frankly, a poor head of department will be happy to offload the thinking onto the first person to make a suggestion. So whether you are a head of department yourself or not, you should be able to take control of any time given to you and use it to further the cause of the revolution: to help everyone teach like nobody's watching. This chapter discusses how department CPD time can be used to make teaching more effective and more efficient.

DEVELOPING SUBJECT KNOWLEDGE

Once a teacher has completed their initial teacher training (ITT) it can be very easy to let the development of subject knowledge slip. Most CPD in schools is, by its very nature, generic and unlikely to focus on improving knowledge in any one subject. There has also been a prevalent belief in education that subject knowledge is less important than knowing how to teach and that a teacher should be able to teach any subject.[2]

However, as we just saw, the research by Robert Coe et al. found that the most important factor affecting pupils' learning was the teacher's subject knowledge, along with the quality of their instruction. A year earlier Coe had published his recommendations for effective CPD, which included a focus on subject-specific CPD.[3] We can also see the importance of subject knowledge in Barak Rosenshine's principles of instruction. As outlined in Chapter 2, he looked at the research into effective teachers and considered what qualities they shared. One finding was that the most effective teachers talked to the class for significantly longer than less effective teachers did. They used this time to explain things carefully, to demonstrate and to model answers. You can't explain, demonstrate and model unless you yourself understand the subject well.

2 See Christodoulou, *Seven Myths About Education*.
3 Coe, Improving Education.

Some teachers are very capable of managing the development of their own subject knowledge (they continue to read around their subject, watch documentaries, visit museums, keep up to date with developments in academia, are members of their subject association, etc.) but everyone's time is limited. I'd suggest that there are three steps which we can take as a department to help everyone work on their subject knowledge.

Step one - audit

Many pupils make a common mistake when it comes to revision. They think about the subject they are going to revise, remember a topic they have studied and then go and revise it. The problem is, the topic that first comes to mind is probably the one they least need to revise. The same is true with developing our own subject knowledge. This is why the first step in developing your department's subject knowledge, and the first activity to complete in any CPD time you have, is to carry out a very honest audit of everyone's strengths and weaknesses. In most subjects, what you learnt during your degree will be much more specialised than what is covered throughout Key Stages 3 and 4, so it is hardly surprising if some teachers have significant gaps in their knowledge.

One key point to remember is that you want this process to be collaborative and open. It is important that everyone understands why you are carrying out an audit and that it is about looking at the strengths and weaknesses of the team, not at them as individuals. One way to achieve this is to start by modelling the process and discussing the gaps in your own knowledge first.

There are a few methods you could use to audit the subject knowledge of your team.

Use the specification

You could copy the exam specification for your course and ask everyone to read it through and highlight any areas of concern. Once this is done, you can look for any areas of overlap and seek to address these first. A pitfall of this approach is that it is human nature to overestimate our knowledge and ability: a phenomenon known as the Dunning-Kruger effect.[4] It can be very easy to read through a specification, recognise what it is asking you to teach and so assume that you have the knowledge with which to do so.

Use exam papers

Another method would be to use past exam papers and ask everyone (yourself included) to sit them, or a selection of questions from them, in exam conditions. Whilst you would hope that everyone would be able to answer the questions, this can highlight which topics people struggle with most as they may have to spend more time thinking about some answers. You can assess which knowledge comes less automatically.

Use the exam results

Your exam board should provide question level analysis from the exams. In many cases this will show how your pupils performed compared to similar centres and the national average. You can often see whether there are particular topics that your pupils struggled with more than others, which might suggest a weakness in the teaching of this topic. This, in turn, might stem from weaker subject knowledge.

Play "Just a Minute"

A more informal and lighthearted way to approach this is to play Just a Minute. Write down different topics from your subject on pieces of paper. People draw them at random and are challenged to speak on that topic for a minute without repetition, hesitation or deviation, in the style of the Radio 4 programme of the same name. Depending on your team, this can be good fun and a quick way to spot what people can speak fluently about and what causes problems.

4 Justin Kruger and David Dunning, Unskilled and unaware of it: how difficulties in recognizing one's own incompetence lead to inflated self-assessments, *Journal of Personality and Social Psychology* 77(6) (1999): 1121–1134.

Step two - address the gaps

Once the audit has been carried out and you have analysed it to look for any gaps, it is time to come up with a plan for how those gaps will be addressed. This won't happen overnight, but is something you will be working on steadily over the years.

Play to your strengths

Don't assume that the head of department will be responsible for delivering any training on improving subject knowledge; this should not be the case. Everyone in the team will have their own strengths - revealed in the audit - that they can share. An NQT might be fresh out of university and very knowledgeable about a new academic aspect of the subject, whilst a teacher who has been in the profession for decades may have taught something that has recently been reintroduced into the exam specification.

Make the first ten minutes of each department meeting a permanent slot in which someone shares their expertise in an aspect of your subject. Come up with a rota at the start of the year so people can fill in what they plan to talk about. This is also an easy way to highlight the experts to go to for anyone who is struggling to teach an aspect of the course.

Use your subject association

Make sure that you are a member of your subject association and make good use of it. Most produce a regular journal with articles relating to developing subject knowledge. Copy these or print them out and dedicate some of your department time to reading and discussing them. Many associations also run evening talks that staff might be able to attend. It is also often possible to host a talk at your own school, for pupils and staff, especially if you invite other schools from your area to create a larger and wider audience.

Book club

Set aside some time in your department meetings to discuss anything subject-related that people are currently reading. This could be books or articles. Encourage everyone to bring material in and share it with their colleagues. It is about slowly shifting the culture and showing that CPD is valued. Widen the remit to include TV shows, radio interviews and websites.

As we discussed in Part I, in his seminal book *Why Don't Students Like School?*, Daniel Willingham points out that "memory is the residue of thought". If we don't think about what we have seen and read, we don't remember it, and the information isn't there to share with our pupils. We need to build in time for reflection and recall if we want this to stick.

Widen the team

There are a huge number of passionate and knowledgeable teachers out there on social media who are discussing their subject and sharing what they know with each other. Many teachers, quite rightly, resent the idea that they need to spend their evenings and weekends glued to Twitter to talk shop, so set aside some department time, once in a while, to have a look at what is being discussed. Most subjects have their own hashtags, so search out #TeamEnglish or #Geographyteacher and see if there is anything useful that can be taken away. Many subjects also have their own regular live chats on Twitter, dedicated to talking about the teaching of different topics. See what you can find.

Step three – adapt

It is important that as the team's subject knowledge is improving there is a change in what is being taught or how. If you have spent time looking at developing theories about plate tectonics, you might need to adapt your lessons to include a focus on ridge push and slab pull, rather than simply on the role of convection currents. If your team have been developing their knowledge of the role of women in Victorian novels, you might want to take another look at how *Great Expectations* is being taught.

There are two simple ways in which to make sure that this adaptation of existing schemes of work takes place. The first is to develop subject knowledge in those topics that are about to be taught, and then to allow this new and improved understanding to filter down to everyone's individual lessons. A less haphazard approach would be to make sure that department CPD sessions are split into two halves. In the first, you develop your subject knowledge as a team and then in the second half you review the schemes of work in which this knowledge would be relevant and make the changes there and then. Which method you use will largely depend on your team and the amount of time you have together.

CURRICULUM DESIGN

For the department to be effective, it is important that each teacher has a very clear understanding of what the curriculum of your subject is setting out to do. Everyone needs to know why one lesson follows another and why one topic follows the one before. We can think of our curriculum as a tapestry in which the individual topic threads come together to form the whole picture. This will only happen if everyone knows what they are trying to weave.

In her 2018 report into the curriculum, Amanda Spielman, Ofsted's chief inspector, commented that "Too many teachers and leaders have not been trained to think deeply about what they want their pupils to learn and how they are going to teach it."[5] Curriculum design is highly subject-specific and so training in "deep thinking" is only likely to happen in department-led CPD.

Reviewing, planning and evaluating the curriculum as a team is an excellent use of department CPD time. It allows you to have those vital professional conversations about the very nature of your subject and how this is translated into what happens in the classroom.

Step one - question

The first step in developing a coherent curriculum as a team is to ask yourselves questions about the curriculum you want, and the one you have got:

- What story do you want your curriculum to tell? Mary Myatt talks about curriculum as a journey that, like a story, takes pupils from where they are,

---

5 Amanda Spielman, HMCI commentary: curriculum and the new education inspection framework (18 September 2018). Available at: https://www.gov.uk/government/speeches/hmci-commentary-curriculum-and-the-new-education-inspection-framework.

through the twists and turns of the plot to a final thrilling dénouement.[6] It isn't a random collection of topics or an exam specification to tick off but a narrative that you are telling. Spend some time as a team exploring what the big questions that your subject attempts to answer are. As Christine Counsell points out, each subject is on its own quest for truth.[7] For geography this might be, "How do natural forces shape the landscape?" For English, "How do writers manipulate language to achieve different effects for their audience?"

- What substantive knowledge is needed for pupils to be able to answer these big questions? This is the content that we teach as established facts. Take one of the big questions that you have identified and mind map the information that someone would need to be able to tackle it.
- What disciplinary knowledge is needed? This is the knowledge of how the substantive knowledge was reached. Which techniques do you need to teach pupils so that they can understand the workings of your subject?
- How should your curriculum be structured? Many programmes of study evolve over time and the original thinking behind the structure becomes lost. Start fresh. What do pupils need to learn first in order to make sense of what comes next? Think back to the discussion in Chapter 5 on Jan Meyer and Ray Land's "threshold concepts": troublesome knowledge that pupils need to grasp before they can move on to anything else. What is the troublesome knowledge in your own subject?
- What are you passionate about? Formal curricula actually allow a huge amount of freedom regarding what is taught. Teachers take the academic discipline and, as Roger Firth explains, recontextualise it.[8] It is an enormous responsibility and a privilege to be the ones who decide what should be passed on to the next generation. Once you have identified the big questions that you want pupils to be able to answer, and the substantive and disciplinary knowledge they will need in order to do so, it is time to fill in the details. Which texts, places, periods or examples do you want to include? What are your team knowledgeable or passionate about?

6 Myatt, *The Curriculum*.

7 Christine Counsell, Taking curriculum seriously, *Impact: Journal of the Chartered College of Teaching* (September 2018). Available at: https://impact.chartered.college/article/taking-curriculum-seriously/.

8 Firth, Recontextualising geography as a school subject.

Step two - map

Once you have spent a department CPD session interrogating your ideas about the curriculum that you want to create, it is time to start mapping it out together. It is important that this is done as a team so that everyone understands what you are trying to achieve and can see the bigger picture. It also means that you can draw on a wider pool of experience in your subject.

Start at the end. What do you want pupils to know, understand and be able to do by the time they leave you? If you work backwards from there you can make sure that all the topics are supporting this end point. Not in an attempt to reduce pupils' whole school lives to preparing them for their GCSEs or A levels, but because it will produce a coherent curriculum with a real end point.

Look back at your answers to the questions in step one. Turn them into topics that you are going to teach. Look at the national curriculum and exam specifications to add in any topics that you feel you haven't already covered. Write each topic on a piece of paper and start shuffling them about. Discuss as a team where each one should go and why. Avoid artificial constraints like making them match up to each term or fit into an assessment schedule. For now, focus on the most sensible way of structuring your curriculum.

Once you have your structure, make sure you record it! Then look at the first topics you will deliver in each key stage. What is the big question for these topics? This big question will sit at the heart of your scheme of work. Decide what you will need to teach in this particular topic. What substantive and disciplinary knowledge will you need to include? What are the threshold concepts? Plan out a rough scheme of work and then divide up the planning. This should be much more achievable now as everyone knows what you are aiming for.

Step three - evaluate

Another useful way to spend department CPD is to evaluate your curriculum as an ongoing process. This way you can check that the curriculum you planned out is the one that is actually being delivered.

One thing to check is that pupils aren't just doing the lessons but are actually learning what you wanted them to learn. As discussed in Chapter 1, one quick way to evaluate this is through regular low-stakes quizzes at the start of lessons. Ask questions that go back over material from previous topics, have pupils mark their own work and record their score in the back of their book. If everyone does the same quizzes in the same week, you can then bring along the results to your next CPD session and see what is sticking and what isn't. You might also be able to identify whether some teachers are having more success with some concepts than others and look at the reasons why. You can do the same with longer pieces of work.

You also need to evaluate the teaching of your new curriculum. How are the team finding it? Is it still making sense? Is there a sense of progress through each lesson or are things starting to drift?

LESSON PLANNING

We can also make good use of department time by planning lessons collaboratively. Once you have gone through the process of agreeing the curriculum and creating a scheme of work, it should be much easier to divide out the content so that each of you doesn't end up planning the same lesson in isolation. It should mean that in a team of four people, you only need to plan and resource 25% of your lessons. This is a much more efficient use of teachers' time and means that each lesson will have more time and thought devoted to it. Everyone benefits.

For a collaborative planning approach to be effective it is vitally important that each person understands what the purpose of the curriculum is, so that you are all planning to the same end. You also need to agree on what makes a lesson effective. If one person in the team doesn't understand the value of recap or effective input, for example, the rest of the team is going to end up spending a lot of time retrofitting their lessons to include these aspects. This is not an insurmountable problem but does mean that you need to set aside some of your department CPD time to embed this common understanding before you start dividing up schemes of work and hoping for the best.

CREATING A COMMON CULTURE

Culture in an organisation or group is often simply defined as "the way we do things around here". A shared idea of how we work allows us to collaborate effectively and create something that is greater than the sum of its parts. "Culture" is the reason why we organise teachers into departments, whether as subject groups in secondary schools or key stages in primary, rather than leaving them to work in isolation.

Creating, or building, a common culture doesn't mean that everyone needs to teach exactly the same thing in exactly the same way, but it does mean sharing some general principles about lesson design, assessment and feedback. If everyone is entrenched in doing things their own way, it makes it impossible to cooperate and share planning. This increases the workload for everyone. The point you want to work towards is one at which anyone in the department can teach a lesson created by another member of the team, and assessment and moderation can be shared out easily and efficiently. Luckily, department CPD time is ideally suited to having the conversations that build this common way of working and allow for meaningful collaboration.

Step one – raising the bar

The first step in building a culture of collaboration is to ensure that everyone expects the same high standards from your pupils. It is worth asking yourself, "Does everyone agree what an excellent piece of work and a typical piece of work look like?" The only way to find out is to ask. Use part of a department CPD session to share the work done in your classes. Ask everyone to bring along some work that they believe to be excellent for a range of age groups and also work that they believe to be typical.

Start with the excellent work. Ask everyone to share what it is that they believe makes this work high quality. What criteria are they using to judge it? See if everyone agrees. Is everyone's work of a similar quality or are there stark differences in what teachers will hold up as gold standard?

Next, look at this excellent work as the years progress. Is excellent work at Key Stage 4 significantly better than at Key Stage 3? If so, why? What can they do in your subject that younger pupils cannot? Even better, if you can, compare the work that they were doing in Key Stage 2 with that in Key Stage 3. If it is largely indistinguishable, are your standards too low? There is a reason why Ofsted called Key Stage 3 "the wasted years": they found that too often there was too little progress made.[9]

Next, move on to the typical work. This is often more telling as it reveals the quality of work that teachers see as acceptable. Would you be happy for a respected peer to see this work? Are you satisfied that this work is typical? What are the differences between the excellent work and this work? Spend some time as a department discussing these questions and how you could close the gap between the excellent and the typical.

The final step here is to agree, as a department, what you think an excellent pupil should be able to do in your subject by the end of Key Stage 3. This will be highly subject-specific so start with what makes your subject unique. What are you aiming for pupils to be able to know or do? Come up with a list. For geography you might have something like:

- Possess and utilise graphical skills.
- Possess and utilise cartographic skills.
- Understand physical processes.
- Substantiate conclusions.

Finally, come up with a statement about what an excellent pupil would be able to do to demonstrate each of these. For example, "An excellent geography pupil will be able to interpret a range of graphs and use them to identify trends. They will be able to use these graphs to make judgements about an issue."

Step two – planning and collaboration

If you get the planning and collaboration right, everyone in the team should be planning a fraction of their own lessons from scratch. You will have a shared understanding of what makes an excellent lesson and can teach using each other's plans

9 Ofsted, *Key Stage 3: The Wasted Years?* Ref: 150106 (September 2015). Available at: https://www.gov.uk/government/publications/key-stage-3-the-wasted-years.

much more readily. When we teach like nobody's watching we can ignore the pernicious myth that diligent teachers plan all of their own lessons and that to use someone else's resources is to somehow shirk your responsibility. Our responsibility is to give our pupils access to the best education we can offer. That education will be much improved if we share out the load and free up time to spend on crafting each lesson.

To do this you need to establish what everyone believes makes an excellent lesson. Draw up a list of all the potential features (group work, silent work, questioning, independence, teacher-talk, etc.). Cut this list up into the individual components and ask each member of your team to organise them from most to least effective along a line. You can increase the complexity of the task by adding a second axis from frequently done to rarely done so that they can organise the features in a matrix. You can find an example from my own department along with the resources to do it yourself on the *Heathfield Teach Share* blog.[10]

Once everyone has done this, ask them to share their thoughts and discuss any differences in opinion. Why do these exist? Does anyone hold any misconceptions about how children learn? Are there differences between how we know we should teach and how we know others want us to teach (those complications from outside)? We want to work out where our attitudes and beliefs about teaching and learning have come from.

Next, consider what the educational research suggests are effective components of a lesson (Part I of this book should give you a great starting point). How much overlap is there between what the research says and what you as teachers say? If there are areas where your views diverge, can you think why this is? What are your own views based on and is it possible that they are wrong? Are you willing to try a different method and see what happens?

By the end of the session, come up with a list of the characteristics you all want to see in a lesson. Ask everyone to plan a lesson that has these characteristics and share it with the team.

In future sessions, you might want to look in more detail at particular features of an excellent lesson, such as Daniel Willingham's work on making lessons memorable

10 Mark Enser, What makes effective learning?, *Heathfield Teach Share* [blog] (19 May 2017). Available at: https://heathfieldteachshare.wordpress.com/2017/05/19/what-makes-effective-learning/.

in *Why Don't Students Like School?*, the importance of threshold concepts from Jan Meyer and Ray Land, Barak Rosenshine's principles of instruction or Robert Coe's work on efficacy.

Step three - motivation

This final step of effective department CPD is hugely important. Subject CPD will only work if everyone is motivated to take part. There are a few points that are worth considering here:

- Leadership is vital in motivation. If the head of department seems lacklustre about the use of this time, they can expect the team to feel the same way.
- Research by David Berliner suggests that experts and novices need teaching in different ways. If we treat expert teachers as novices, they will progress more slowly. Experts need less direct instruction and more collaborative coaching, through which they are prompted to find solutions to problems for themselves.[11]
- Each session should have a clear aim, shared with the team. The review questions throughout this chapter have been designed to help you reflect on the purpose of these activities.
- Department CPD almost always comes at the end of a long teaching day. Ideally everyone will have time to grab a coffee, someone will bring biscuits and, if possible, you can find somewhere comfortable to sit and talk - it doesn't have to be in a classroom.

11 David Berliner, Expert teachers: their characteristics, development and accomplishments. In I. Batllori, R. Obiols, A. E. Gomez Martinez, M. Oller, I. Freixa, J. Pages and I. Blanch (eds), *De la teoria ... a l'aula: Formacio del professorat ensenyament de las ciències socials* (Barcelona: Departament de Didàctica de la Llengua i la Literatura, i de les Ciències Socials, Universitat Autònoma de Barcelona, 2004), pp. 13-28. Available at: https://www.researchgate.net/profile/David_Berliner2/publication/255666969_Expert_Teachers_Their_Characteristics_Development_and_Accomplishments/links/02e7e53c6d5e6b68d7000000/Expert-Teachers-Their-Characteristics-Development-and-Accomplishments.pdf.

OVERCOMING THE BARRIERS

Hopefully this chapter has shown that department CPD time can be taken back from the demands of whole-school leadership and put to use by teachers on the ground. However, there are potential barriers to the effective use of this time.

What about all the other work we need to do in department CPD time?

Department time has often been used for a whole range of admin tasks. Putting data onto systems, work scrutiny, dealing with rewards systems, filling in surveys for members of the SLT - the list is endless. These are yet more examples of those things that are done primarily for outside audiences. They overcomplicate teaching and also leave little time for quality CPD. To overcome this barrier, you need to be very clear with your line manager about what you are trying to achieve in this time. Look at the other calls on your time and discuss what can be left or done later.

Ideally, of course, many of these tasks are things we would simply not do at all, but at the very least much of it can be done outside of department CPD sessions - for example, they can be achieved through sending a weekly email giving information and asking for certain tasks to be completed. The time saved by collaborating on planning will leave teachers with a bit extra that can be used for non-negotiable tasks.

We don't have much department time. When can we do all of this?

Hopefully schools are making time for departments to run CPD. If they aren't, and you don't have regular meetings, this does become much more difficult. There are a few potential solutions. Firstly, have a look at the directed time budget in your school. What are they using teachers' time for? Make a case for turning some of this over to departments.

Secondly, see if you can get several teachers in your department off timetable for a training session several times a year - even if only for an hour at a time. Point out to your CPD coordinator that this will be a lot cheaper than sending people on expensive external courses.

Finally, and far from ideally, make use of electronic communication. Work on things using email and shared documents. Share articles this way and discuss your reading as and when you can.

Not everyone in my team is on board. What should I do about them?

Sadly, not every teacher sees the value in CPD. This is, in part, because so much of it has had little value. Find out what their specific concerns are. It could be that they are completely justified and you need to rethink how the time is being used.

You can try to bring everyone on board by being very clear about what you are trying to achieve and why you think this time is going to be valuable. Showing that you really have thought this through will hopefully allay many fears. Finally, explain how using department time to collaborate will lead to reduced workload for everyone and free up time for other things. This almost always goes down well!

I'm not sure that I have the subject knowledge I need to develop it in others. What can I do?

One serious problem with handing over CPD time to heads of department is making sure that they have the ability to develop their team. Who trains the trainers? There are a number of solutions to this issue.

Firstly, remember that you don't need to develop all of the CPD yourself if you are the head of department. A great use of department time is to share each other's areas of expertise. You could even do this between a local hub of schools and so increase the potential pool of in-depth subject knowledge. Secondly, you can make use of your subject association to improve your own subject knowledge by reading more deeply around the areas on which you know the department needs to work. Exam specifications often have guides to teaching aspects of the course, especially if it is something new. Finally, be clear that you are on this journey together. You are all trying to develop your knowledge, and no one should feel that they can't admit to their weaknesses.

How can we collaborate when everyone teaches differently and has different needs?

Although everyone may have a different style of teaching, the basic principles of what makes an effective lesson are the same (recap, input, application and feedback). Spend more time exploring these principles together.

In terms of people having different needs, this is where a well-planned CPD programme comes in. Make sure that everyone's needs are being addressed over the year. Some people may be brushing up on something they are already competent at whereas other people may be considering it for the first time. This is not a problem and it leads to far richer discussions.

KEY POINTS

- Teachers can take back ownership of what they are doing in school by seizing control of any department CPD time. Kick out as much admin as you can and focus on things that will make your teaching more effective and efficient.
- By building a common culture we can create an environment in which it is much easier to collaborate and share lesson planning.
- As well as building a common culture, it helps if everyone has been involved in the discussions around curriculum planning. Everyone needs to understand the journey on which they are taking their pupils.
- Few things will have as much of an immediate impact on the quality and ease of teaching as improving subject knowledge. Reading is a perfectly reasonable use of meeting time.
- We can also improve subject knowledge using the existing expertise within our teams by spending time teaching each other about aspects of the curriculum.

REFLECTIONS

- What was your last department meeting used for? Who set what items on the agenda? Who benefitted from each item?
- If you were free to set the agenda yourself, what would you do with the time?
- Who in your department is an expert on what subject area?
- What would you say is the purpose of your curriculum? Do you think everyone in your department would give the same answer? Does this matter?
- Is everyone in your department at the same point on the continuum from novice to expert? Do different teachers need different levels of support in this process?

PART III
THE WIDER SCHOOL

INTRODUCTION TO PART III

As I hope is clear by now, I am a firm believer that there is a huge amount that the individual teacher can do to reclaim what happens in their classroom. If we are knowledgeable about effective and efficient ways in which to teach, we can embrace these methods, shut out much of the nonsense that is thrown our way and teach like nobody's watching.

However, I acknowledge that this is much easier to do in some schools than in others. It is hard to teach in an effective and efficient manner if various members of the SLT arrive at your door clutching their own latest batch of "non-negotiables" or if your lesson is spent battling disruptive behaviour with no support. This is why this final part considers what school leaders can do to help create the conditions which will allow us to teach like nobody's watching.

There is an old saying that people don't leave jobs, they leave managers. And in the case of teaching, leave they certainly do. Our present culture, which lacks professional trust and creates an unsustainable workload, is leading to teachers fleeing our schools.[1] A cold-hearted observer may conclude that this is fine as long as there are teachers available to replace those we lose. This, however, is not the case. Teacher training courses are undersubscribed in many subjects and the teachers

1 Louise Tickle, "Every lesson is a battle": why teachers are lining up to leave, *The Guardian* (10 April 2018). Available at: https://www.theguardian.com/education/2018/apr/10/lesson-battle-why-teachers-lining-up-leave.

arriving in the classroom are, of course, less experienced and less effective than those leaving. It is also expensive to train and recruit new teachers. The whole situation is unsustainable, and something needs to change.

There are many excellent books out there on school leadership written by school leaders. Here, though, we'll look at the issue of whole-school leadership from my perspective as a classroom teacher who spends a lot of time talking to and working with other classroom teachers. There are many wonderful schools out there whose leaders are addressing the challenge of creating a culture of professional autonomy when the wider culture calls for high-stakes accountability. I have included case studies from some of these schools in the hope of proving that there is another way: a way of giving teachers the professional agency to get on and do their jobs.

CHAPTER 9

LEADERS SUPPORTING TEACHING

WELL-BEING

It is always heartening to see school leaders take the issue of teacher retention seriously and many schools have embraced this with a range of well-being initiatives. These include things like mindfulness activities or yoga sessions during INSET days, cakes in the staffroom on a Friday, nomination systems to recognise teachers for their achievements, and healthy eating initiatives.

The problem is that, however well intentioned, they don't tackle the underlying causes of poor teacher well-being: high workload and stress. These kinds of activities might be the icing on the cake, but if the sponge is rotten, the icing does little to make it more appealing. If we really want to deal with teacher well-being, we need to reduce the workload. This will then give us the time to do yoga, eat a cake or shop for healthy food. The school doesn't need to do any of these things if they get workload right.

This chapter looks at some of the things school leaders can do to truly improve well-being from a teacher's perspective - without a yoga mat in sight.

BEHAVIOUR

The teacher surveying app TeacherTapp has revealed an interesting difference in views about behaviour between teachers on the ground and senior leaders.[1] Senior leaders regard poor behaviour as much less of a problem in their schools than the teachers do. This is worrying as it suggests that managing poor behaviour will not be given the priority it needs by these leaders. It is teachers in the earliest stages of their careers who are most likely to report that poor behaviour is a problem and a source of stress.[2] These are the very people who are most likely to leave the profession and the ones we most need to support.

It is almost impossible to teach well in a class that is being disrupted by poor behaviour. Let's think about the things that won't happen:

- Pupils are unable to concentrate during retrieval practice. If they aren't thinking about their previous learning, this won't work.
- The teacher's explanation gets interrupted and the pupils' lines of thought are disturbed. This will mean the explanation won't stick when they try to apply it.
- Disruption during the application of what they have learnt means pupils aren't fully concentrating on the content. We remember what we think about.
- The teacher can't circulate the class to monitor independent practice and give feedback if their time is spent trying to keep some pupils on task.

Recap, input, application, feedback: all these critical parts of a lesson are affected. It won't matter how good your curriculum is – if the teacher can't deliver it, nothing will be learnt. Therefore, it is imperative that if leaders want teachers to teach, they need to do everything they can to support a culture of excellent behaviour in the school.

One way to achieve this is to make sure that the school's behaviour policy is easy to follow and time efficient. Some policies act as a perverse disincentive for teachers to deal with disruption as they require them to fill in paperwork, make a phone call

1 Laura McInerney, Behaviour: what is really going on in schools? *TeacherTapp* [blog] (10 February 2019). Available at: http://teachertapp.co.uk/2019/02/behaviour-what-is-really-going-on-in-schools-2019/.
2 Laura McInerney, What teachers tapped this week #50, *TeacherTapp* [blog] (10 September 2018). Available at: http://teachertapp.co.uk/2018/09/what-teachers-tapped-this-week-50-10th-september/.

home to discuss the poor behaviour, and find the time to have a restorative conversation and a detention with the pupil. If you were a teacher with a five-period day and a meeting after school, would you follow this process or let the disruptive pupil off with a warning and hope that they will magically improve before the next lesson? If the former, when would you find the time to follow the policy and what would you spend less time doing instead?

If teachers are to follow a behaviour policy, it has to be possible for them to do so. Centralised detentions mean that sanctions can be delivered in a more efficient manner, with just a couple of staff needed to supervise everyone's detentions on any given afternoon. Contact home can be made electronically or by someone in the admin team and teachers can have conversations about behaviour at a time they judge to be most appropriate.

CASE STUDY: BEHAVIOUR AND CULTURE

Barry Smith, Headmaster, Great Yarmouth Charter Academy

Charter is built on genuine mutual respect. Adults teach pupils to be very polite. It's a key part of our job. We model, very explicitly and very consistently, what "normal for Charter" means. It's a habitual "morning, miss!" or "thanks, sir!" It's habitually greeting everyone in a smiley, upbeat manner: very often a handshake, pretty much always a smile. That's us, the adults, talking to kids. We "sir" and "miss" the kids a lot.

We are - very demonstrably - courteous, welcoming and positive. We expect exactly the same level of consistent courtesy back. We insist that all adults are treated with respect. That goes across the board. As a consequence, midday supervisors, cleaners and supply teachers all know they're valued and respected as a key part of the Charter team. Charter kids are polite to everyone.

At the hint of anything less than the utmost courtesy, we remind pupils, "That's somebody's mum. That's somebody's dad. They work hard for you. Without them, Charter wouldn't exist and we'd go back to how the school was before Charter."[3]

Similarly, we regularly remind pupils how lucky they are to have the teachers they do. "Your teachers' words are gold dust! They've got degrees, master's, PhDs. They've taught thousands and thousands of pupils. Every break time, every lunchtime, every lesson changeover, every morning at the gate, every evening at the gate, across the road in the park, they're there for you."

We tell the kids, "Why do you think we get so many visitors? Why do you think visitors come from across the country and abroad to see you? It's because there's nowhere else like Charter. All of these teachers and head teachers, they keep asking, 'How come your kids are so polite? How come they're so focused and hard-working? How come they're so confident? How come your teachers teach with such energy? How come your teachers are everywhere at every lesson changeover?' Charter is about an attitude of gratitude. What are you? You are Charter-tastic! We're so proud of you. When visitors come to the school, you blow them away - every single time - with your superb manners, your confidence, your smart appearance, your 'good morning, miss!', your handshakes, your projection, your full sentences, your eye contact."

We've created a culture in which everybody supports everybody else. We know that if we're slack, we're letting our colleagues down, someone else is having to work twice as hard to carry us.

And if we slacken, if we don't support each other? We know that the bad old days could come back in a heartbeat. Why does Charter work? We've known the very worst of times, we took back our self-respect, and now we know the joy of really teaching, of teamwork, of banter, of camaraderie with the kids and with colleagues. We know how bad things can get and we know that only genuine mutual respect can save us from going back there.

3 The school that became Great Yarmouth Charter Academy was one of the worst performing schools in the country.

Takeaway points:

- There needs to be a consistent approach to behaviour so that there isn't a two-tier culture of teachers for whom pupils behave and those for whom they misbehave.
- Pupils should feel proud of their school and believe in what they are trying to achieve.
- If leaders don't actively work to maintain standards, they will soon slip.

TRACKING

We desire many things of data, but that does not mean that what we want to show is possible. It would be very useful to be able to give pupils a number to say, "This is where they are in their attainment" and it would be good if this allowed national comparisons. It would also be really useful to be able to predict the qualifications a child would go on to get. This information would be desirable for pupils, parents, teachers and leaders alike. They could use it to inform planning and make very accurate assessments of who might benefit most from additional support.

The problem is that, however desirable it might be to pinpoint current attainment and make predictions based on that, it isn't possible to do so. As we saw in Chapter 7, a huge amount of teachers' time and energy is spent trying to make the impossible possible and all that is produced is a lot of junk data that we then use to make flawed decisions. Summative grading judgements create the illusion of meaningful data, but, as we discussed, trying to conflate assessment results into GCSE grades is deeply problematic.

A further problem is that we assume that grades convey a shared and definitive meaning, which they actually do not. Even if we take the final GCSE result itself, the marking of papers in many subjects (English and history in particular, but few are immune) is highly subjective and Ofqual's own research shows that only 55% of markers agree with the principal examiner when awarding a final grade in some subjects.[4] When a pupil receives a 5 in English, we should be aware that this could

4 For a full exploration of this research see Alex Ford, Examinations: the gilded age, *And All That* [blog] (7 March 2019). Available at: http://www.andallthat.co.uk/blog/examinations-the-gilded-age.

just as easily have been a 4 or a 6. In fact, there is a 4% chance that it could have been a 3 or a 7.[5] And these are papers marked by people who are specifically trained to do so and with moderation in place. What hope has the teacher in the classroom got?

As we saw in Chapter 7, the problem actually gets much worse. These grades are generated from grade boundaries set after the exam has been taken based on how the cohort did, to take into account the shifting difficulty of the papers year on year. GCSE grade boundaries certainly can't be applied to exams that teachers have created for themselves unless the person writing it has somehow ensured that their paper is the exact same difficulty as the original papers that year – something even professional exam paper writers can't do. Nor can you take the grade boundaries from a past paper and apply them to the results of a new cohort, unless the whole paper is sat in the same conditions as it was originally. If you do anything that makes that exam easier to score on (such as only doing one topic, directing revision, not having several high-stakes exams in the same week, etc.) the grade boundaries would need to shift.

A school is judged on how pupils do against the targets that they are set based on their Key Stage 2 results. This means that as soon as a pupil arrives in Year 7, the school can work out what their target grade should be in five years' time. They then ask teachers to regularly predict whether pupils are on track to reach it. This is even more problematic than trying to pinpoint current attainment because progress is not linear: pupils might seem to make rapid progress at certain points and plateau at others. How a pupil is doing midway through Year 8 tells us nothing about their likely achievement at the end of Year 11.

In many schools, teachers are judged on the data they enter into tracker sheets during the school year. Teachers or departments whose data shows pupils performing badly may see themselves monitored more heavily and forced to justify the results they have given. Since teachers are well aware that the data is all made up, it is hardly surprising they just make up different data to keep school leaders happy. If school leaders want to create conditions in which teachers can thrive (and I sincerely believe that they do) we need them to stop asking the impossible. We need to be honest about what data can and can't tell us and stop chasing impossible dreams.

---

5 I worked out these figures from the statistics given in Ford's blog post.

CASE STUDY: USE OF RANK ORDER ASSESSMENT

Stephen Adcock, Deputy Director of Secondary Academies, United Learning

Next time you see a school report, take it to the first non-educationalist you can find - perhaps your next-door neighbour - and kindly ask them to explain it back to you. It might not do much for neighbourly relations, but you'll soon realise that a typical report makes little sense to those who don't spend their days in schools.

Now imagine that instead of reference to arbitrary grades and expected progress, the report revealed how each pupil performed in relation to the rest of the year group - for example, 17/180 in English, 25/180 in maths, and 70/180 in French. Your neighbour might make sense of this.

In simple terms, rank order (or "relative performance" if the rank bit sounds too brutal) means that at given points in their schooling, let's say twice a year, pupils sit a test in each of their subjects. It's a standardised test, so the whole year group sits the same test in the same conditions. Once the marks and percentages are totted up, pupils are told how they performed in relation to their peers in each subject.

Rank orders provide clarity. Over time, pupils see whether their performance in each subject is improving or declining in relation to their peers. This is powerful stuff - more powerful than giving pupils an abstract working-at grade based on a teacher's best guess of what a grade 5 at the end of Year 11 might look like halfway through Year 8 (in a different topic!).

There's a hidden benefit to rank orders: they ensure that all pupils follow the same curriculum because teachers know that at fixed points in the year all pupils will be assessed on the same stuff. This can be especially powerful for pupils in lower sets, who too often find themselves following an inferior curriculum to their higher attaining peers.

Rank order will only ever be one part of the assessment mix, and I'm always keen to stress how infrequently pupils receive information of this kind. Their daily diet of feedback will always be in the moment, in the class, from their teachers. But I think that rank order has its place in this mix, and can provide a bracing clarity which is sorely lacking from other ways of describing pupil performance.

A frequent criticism of rank order assessment is that there will always be pupils in the bottom half of the rank, and that it's harsh to remind them that they are not performing as well as their peers. I get this, and as with most school policies I think the success should be judged by its impact on our most vulnerable pupils. But when they collect their GCSE results at the end of Year 11, all pupils will find out in pretty stark terms how they did in relation to their peers throughout the country. Rank order can help put pupils in the driving seat by revealing how they're doing compared to their peers at a point when they can still do something about it.

Ultimately, different forms of assessment serve different purposes. Sometimes we want to know which parts of the course pupils are better or worse at; sometimes we want to know how our pupils are doing compared to national standards. And sometimes we want to reveal to pupils with as much clarity as possible how they are doing across the curriculum. Rank order assessment can help us do this.

Takeaway points:

- Rank order assessment takes away some of the guesswork about what a score "means". There is an honesty about it.
- Using rank order assessment also means that everyone *has* to be entitled to the same curriculum so that everyone can do the same assessment.
- Rank order assessment is ultimately what happens in the exam. Exposing pupils to this during their time at school gives them the information whilst they can do something about it.

NON-NEGOTIABLES

Making something a non-negotiable - adding it to those lists of things that school leaders expect to see in every lesson - is possibly the quickest way to kill off a good idea. It is understandable how this happens. This book has, I hope, shown that there are several things that good teachers should probably be doing: recapping previous learning, asking a range of questions, giving time for independent practice, and giving timely feedback. It is tempting to put these things on a piece of paper, attach it to a clipboard and then go and make sure you can see these things happening in every lesson.

The problem is that this creates cargo cult lessons. Cargo cults arose in the Pacific Islands in the early 20th century. The indigenous inhabitants had seen western explorers land planes on their newly made airstrips and offload all kinds of exciting cargo. When these western travellers left, the cargo went with them. The islanders wanted this cargo back and so built planes and airstrips from bamboo in the hope that this would lead to the cargo returning. They had seen the structure but missed the detail. They had the what but not the why.

This is the danger that school leaders create when issuing lists of non-negotiables. They may be followed but if there is no understanding of the underlying principle, they are unlikely to be effective. For example, we know that linking a lesson to previous learning is important and that many teachers do this through retrieval quizzes at the start of the lesson. It might, therefore, seem desirable for leaders to say, "We expect to see retrieval quizzes at the start of a lesson." But it's not as simple as that. There are good and bad ways to organise a quick quiz - and issues to address around keeping them low stakes, question selection and how to provide feedback. Simply issuing the edict that leaders expect to see them is likely to lead to a lot of poor-quality quizzes until the idea is eventually abandoned as something that isn't having impact.

We are currently seeing something similar happening with whole-class feedback. As discussed in Part I, whole-class feedback can be a very effective and efficient way of making sure that pupils know how to improve. Many school leaders are very aware of the impact that marking policies are having on teachers and are therefore looking for alternatives. Whole-class feedback seems to fit the bill. The problem comes when you make it the expectation, something you want evidence of, as the best whole-class feedback doesn't leave much of a trace. Feedback from one piece of work is applied to something else and you can't precisely trace the evolution of the pupil's work. The result has been that teachers have been asked to print off templates that they can use to record this feedback and have pupils stick these into their books. This immediately makes the idea less efficient and creates a needless layer of work just to make something visible to an outside observer.

Non-negotiables may be imposed with the best of motives, but they inevitably distort teacher practice. A better approach would be to introduce teachers to the underlying ideas behind the things leaders would like to see and to discuss a range of strategies that would allow their implementation. And then leave teachers to it.

CASE STUDY: PROFESSIONAL TRUST

Sam Gorse, Head Teacher, Turton School

Starting from the assumption that teachers are intelligent adults who want to do a good job, and make a difference, we believe that school improvement comes from everyone getting a bit better every year. This involves great teachers pushing their practice into the margins, and growing teachers gaining strength from incremental improvements – safe in the knowledge that developing their performance is permitted organically, free from targets and rigid timescales. The whole school works together, collaboratively, to enable each individual to improve their practice, thus fulfilling our collective ambition for school improvement.

We reject the notion of performance-related pay and have discarded the term "performance management". Instead, we have a collaborative approach to development, which we call our Triad process. Through this, staff work together on "intentions" for the year (not targets) – things they have identified as having the potential to improve their classroom practice. All intentions are classroom based, no matter your level of responsibility, because this is the place where improvement is most impactful and the place where we are all equal in our pursuit of excellence.

Through the Triad process, staff have the freedom and support to research, experiment and evidence their developments. This is underpinned by the belief that it is just as valuable to publicly demonstrate how something may not have had the desired impact as it is to celebrate those things that work well.

If we assume that teachers are intelligent adults, who want to make a difference, then we do not need systems and structures to control them. We simply need to teach them about our vision and ethos, and offer them the climate and support that enables them to improve their practice, bit by bit, day by day. In a collaborative culture like ours, we are constantly teaching each other about what we do. Everyone is an expert and everyone is a novice: we can all teach the things we are good at and learn new things from one another.

We believe that everyone should be able to handle feedback. Hearing feedback is always easier if it is the truth. We speak the truth in feedback – good and bad – with clarity, and people respond by getting better at what they do. Giving feedback has to be practised regularly and given in the moment. The SLT and I do not conduct any lesson observations. We have developed an embedded practice of learning walks, which we discuss as a group and then feed back. All feedback, both general and to individuals, is delivered in an enquiring manner, intended to open up discussion and further reflection.

We create an open learning community, in which giving and receiving feedback is commonplace. My expectation is that the SLT live out our values by making their own learning open and public. You cannot say that you are an open and collaborative learning community and then berate staff if they make a mistake or show that they need to develop in some way. Equally we must operate within a climate of optimism for the future by constantly acknowledging how far the whole community has come. Whole-school development is our ambition, with each of us a contributor to this. Optimism for the future comes from the feeling of working for a cause greater than ourselves, and a belief in our capacity, as a group, to improve.

I refuse to get drawn into offering retention payments and persuading people to stay at Turton, nor do I offer financial incentives to attract candidates to vacancies. Everyone is paid following a straightforward and equitable salary structure. My purpose here is that Turton is known as a great place to be *from* as well as work at. In this way, rather than desperately trying to hold on to people, everyone who leaves becomes an ambassador, not only for Turton - who we are and how we operate - but also for the profession and how it can operate at its best for teachers.

Takeaway points:

- Teachers need to receive feedback, but this needs to be delivered in an enquiring and discursive manner.
- Teachers need the chance to collaborate with their peers in order to develop.
- This ongoing process of collaboration and feedback can only operate in a culture of trust.

CPD

CPD should be something that every teacher values as an important part of their role. A year's teacher training doesn't produce the finished article and we are able to make significant improvements to our practice over the first few years in the job, as long as we are given the time, space and support to reflect and adapt. After these first few years in the classroom, it is very easy for a teacher to plateau. This phenomenon is discussed by Rebecca Allen and Sam Sims, who show that teachers make rapid progress in their first three years of teaching (when thrown in at the deep end and expected, to a great extent, to sink or swim) but then the progress slows to marginal gains.[6] This is despite all teachers continuing to receive something that calls itself CPD. Why doesn't this CPD lead to the development that it is supposed to?

A good starting point when trying to identify what is going wrong is to ask the teachers. The TeacherTapp app did just this and found that a large proportion felt

6 Rebecca Allen and Sam Sims, *The Teacher Gap* (Abingdon: Routledge, 2018).

that the CPD they received offered them nothing of use.[7] This could be because most things that schools call "CPD" are nothing of the sort. I have spent too many hours over the years sat in a draughty school hall whilst each member of the SLT stood up and justified their job as we sat there trying to plan lessons in our heads. The deputy head standing up to talk you through the school's data is not in fact CPD, nor is a talk from the assistant head on attendance, nor, I hate to say it, is the head teacher's vision for the school. All of these speeches might contain useful messages and be important for communication but to call them CPD muddies the waters and means that genuine development may not happen.

A second problem is that most of what is called CPD tends to be very much one-size-fits-all and quite generic. There may be a CPD session after school on questioning, but did all staff need this input? Did the advice apply to all subjects? If not, why is everyone sat there? This problem is complicated still further because teachers at different stages in their careers need very different types of development. As David Berliner explains, novice teachers need far more explicit instruction on how to improve, with concrete examples that they can try to apply in their own practice.[8] Expert teachers, in contrast, have years of experience to fall back on. They can probably work out for themselves how to improve an aspect of their teaching by reflecting on what they already know. For this reason, Berliner suggests that experts may take longer to reach a conclusion but that this conclusion is likely to be better. If a new idea is being introduced, the expert teacher can work out how to apply it to their practice themselves, whereas a novice would need more support.

So where does this leave us? Firstly, I would suggest that CPD needs to be much more bespoke. If you have identified that an aspect of teaching needs to be developed, then target this at those who need it. Don't make 60 teachers sit through a session going back over questioning unless either you have something new to say about it or they genuinely all need to develop this.

Secondly, focus whole-school input on the "why" of the idea. Why do we need to ask different questions at different times? Why might whole-class feedback be a good alternative to written comments? Why is retrieval practice important? Include a few examples of how this might be put in place but then leave it up to

7 Laura McInerney, What teachers tapped this week #56, *TeacherTapp* [blog] (22 October 2018). Available at: http://teachertapp.co.uk/2018/10/what-teachers-tapped-this-week-56-22nd-october-2018/.

8 David Berliner, Learning about and learning from expert teachers, *International Journal of Educational Research* 35 (2001): 463–482.

departments to work how to best apply it to their subjects and classes. The expert teachers should be able to guide the novices and the discussions should be all the richer for this. Outcomes are more likely to be put in place, and then be successful, if everyone understands the principles behind them.

Finally, remember that CPD doesn't just mean teachers gathering in the school hall to be told things. Leaders should give teachers time to read and reflect, time for them to meet and discuss educational research and/or practice. Leaders should make time for teachers to carry out their own small-scale research into innovations to see what is actually effective in their classroom. They could also fund memberships of subject associations and help with the cost of tickets to conferences. All of this will be better value than hiring in a consultant to talk about their latest big idea.

CASE STUDY: CPD AND HOLDING FIRM

Zoe Enser, Director of Improvement and CPD, A Multi-Academy Trust

Working in a school which had faced a number of challenges made us vulnerable in a number of ways.[9] Often we were buffeted by the winds of local authority initiatives, battered by the pedagogical tempests of the Department for Education and vulnerable to even the slightest gusts from passing exam boards. As a result, CPD could sometimes feel removed from the day-to-day practice in our school, and it could be difficult to develop a cohesive strategy on which to hang the ideas. Teaching staff and leaders were exhausted trying to anticipate where the next barrage would come from and which direction it would leave us facing.

On being given the focus for whole-school CPD just under three years ago, my first aim was to provide clarity and structure to firmly underpin what we wanted to achieve with teaching and learning. Reflecting on feedback from external visitors and discussions with other leaders, as well as what had proven

9 This school serves a coastal community with relatively high levels of deprivation.

successful in other schools, such as Durrington High in Worthing, I devised a series of "pillars" on which to base the work of the coming years. These included subject knowledge and pedagogy, the key focus in all we do; stretch and challenge, one of our most pressing issues; independence and resilience, something which would undoubtedly make our job much easier and a prize much sought after; and feedback and marking, an area which we knew could be powerful but was currently drawing a lot of energy from staff with little obvious yield.

Having devised these pillars, I worked with the teaching staff to explore what these areas currently looked like in their subjects and what they would envisage them to look like all things being perfect. A range of activities allowed teachers to work together both in their subject areas and across the curriculum, to explore how others were developing. This included some staff sharing their good practice across the whole staff in longer INSET sessions. Alongside this, research from beyond the school was introduced so teachers could see what was working elsewhere and how this could be applied in our context, where appropriate. Staff were beginning to see how CPD could be driven and controlled by us and a culture of change began to take place.

In the next phase, following discussions with a United Learning colleague, who had been part of a Dylan Wiliam and EEF research project, I introduced Teaching and Learning Communities (TLCs) into the school. The pillars remained and were focused upon in department areas – for example, with subject areas specifically exploring feedback and marking and devising their own policies – but the focus of the TLCs was stretch and challenge across the school. Eight sessions, delivered across the year, shared key research into how topics such as metacognition and questioning could be employed to stretch and challenge all pupils. Staff read or watched the research provided, discussed how it could relate to their own context and agreed a focus with their TLC partner. This partner would then observe it in practice and then the two would feed back, discuss and reflect using a series of prompts.

The eighth session took the form of a TeachMeet, during which each TLC group fed back to the whole staff about their experiences across the year, including what hadn't worked as well as what had. We don't want to continue doing something which is not having an impact. Every member of the teaching staff contributed to this, regardless of their experience or position in the school.

This year, the TLCs have continued with a longer-term focus. Staff signed up to their area of interest at the end of the previous year, in discussion with their line manager, to ensure that they were sharply focused on what they wanted to develop and why. The areas were selected to build on what we had looked at previously and linked to Barak Rosenshine's principles of instruction, which I had also begun to explore with the staff. Each group maintained this focus for the first two terms of the year, exploring research supplied by me, but increasingly with others bringing research to the table, feeling more confident in how to access this. The same model applied and lots of peer observations were undertaken. The fourth session was delivered as a TeachMeet, and each group shared their experiences and next steps.

Following on from this, staff have returned to their subject areas to explore how they can embed some of the best practice within their teams. Smaller departments - such as computer science and RE - joined up with sympathetic departments, to enable them to have richer discussions about the topics. This also built upon a cross-school INSET which had focused on subject areas developing effective instruction across four schools.

Over the past two and a half years, this has led to a culture in which people are focused on discussing teaching and learning as never before. There is clarity in what we are all trying to achieve, and staff are afforded the time to have discussions about what does and does not work in their classrooms. This time is built into our directed time budget, and even allows for feedback from observations so staff are not trying to snatch a few minutes over a hurried lunch to talk. It is important that people really sit and reflect.

More recently I have narrowed our focus as we become clearer on what is working in our context and have the space to refine it. We still use the pillars, and additional time has been given to subject teams to allow that first pillar of subject knowledge the gravitas it deserves. All meetings have CPD at their heart and admin is consigned to email, where it belongs.

Now it feels like we are in a much stronger position to stand firm against any prevailing winds. There is always more to do but staff are braver when talking about why their practice works, and indeed why some things don't. We won't be shaken from our vision of good, research-informed practice, even when faced with the Anemoi of Ofsted.

Takeaway points:

- Whole-school CPD needs to be carefully planned around priorities for the school's development, or we risk only reacting to the latest craze or threat.
- Staff need to "buy in" to whole-school CPD and understand its value and their role in school improvement.
- Subject-specific input is important if more generic CPD is to have an impact.

FEEDBACK POLICIES

As discussed in Part I, workload is driving teachers out of the profession and a leading contributing factor to this high workload is marking. From a teacher's perspective, one of the most maddening things that school leaders can do is insist that teachers mark books every X number of weeks. A survey by TeacherTapp found that 43% of teachers were expected to mark books every two weeks.[10] This is crazy for a number of reasons:

- **It shows a lack of understanding about your own curriculum design.** Saying that books should be marked every X number of weeks is utterly bizarre when different subjects are timetabled differently. Why are English books being marked every eight lessons and geography books every three? In some schools, RE books may be marked after every lesson. What is the rationale for this? I would suggest there isn't one and that it is just lazy leadership.

10 Laura McInerney, How often are teachers expected to mark work?, *TeacherTapp* [blog] (November 2017). Available at: http://teachertapp.co.uk/2017/11/often-teachers-required-mark-work/.

- **It shows a lack of understanding about workload.** Teachers in non-core subjects can easily have ten different classes on their timetable. To fulfil this policy, the teacher would have to mark at least one class set of books every work day, and sometimes more than one. Even on days when they are teaching all five periods. Even on days with a meeting or parents' evening after school. It simply isn't possible to keep up with this directive for long, and the pressure to try is driving people out of the profession.
- **It shows a lack of understanding about feedback.** Feedback is vitally important. It may be one of the most important elements of successful teaching. Feedback is not the same as marking. Writing comments in pupils' books may at times be the most effective way of giving feedback, but it often won't be (see Chapter 4 for more on this). The problem with insisting that books are marked with written comments every two weeks is that other forms of feedback don't happen as everyone is worrying about complying with this directive. Giving immediate written feedback may actually be harmful to progress as it prevents pupils from developing self-regulation.
- **It shows a lack of understanding about the "why".** This is another example of cargo cult teaching: focusing on a practice and not a reason. A policy that states how often books should be marked inevitably ignores why books should be marked. The purpose of feedback becomes lost as people desperately try to keep up with the workload. Comments become generic, feedback is not acted upon and, as a result, we can't adjust our teaching. We end up going through the age-old ritual of marking books whilst the reason for doing so goes unexplored.
- **It shows a lack of understanding about professionalism.** The reason why policies stipulate how often books should be marked is to make it possible to check that it is being done. Marking is therefore done for an audience that isn't the pupil. It becomes yet another "non-negotiable" on the checklist used to monitor teachers. This isn't how you treat a professional. If a leader had any faith in their staff, they would spend time exploring the why of feedback and then leave their professionals to ensure that effective feedback was given. A policy insisting that books are marked every two weeks reeks of distrust and a belief that teachers can't work out how best to do their jobs.

Luckily, this issue is easily solved. Get rid of the policy on marking and instead focus on effective feedback strategies, as discussed in Chapter 4.

CASE STUDY: FEEDBACK AND RESPONSIVE TEACHING

Kate Owbridge, Executive Head Teacher, and Tom Angus, Key Stage 2 Teacher, Ashdown Primary School

Kate: We'd already cut weekly planning for Key Stages 1 and 2 and were using a five-minute lesson plan straight from our schemes of work. We'd also cut marking but it was still a huge burden. The SLT looked at Clare Sealy's whole-class feedback policy and format.[11] We'd just had an Ofsted inspection and one of our target actions was to challenge the most able more effectively. One of Clare Sealy's main points is that the next step is the next lesson. So, through debate and discussion, the SLT decided that if we kept the main elements of whole-class feedback notes (children who needed further challenge, children who needed support, and general notes - misconceptions, common errors, etc.) we could combine it with the next learning steps for those groups of children (fluid groups, which could easily change every lesson) and plan responsively for each child. Teachers had to plan for every child's next learning step, albeit as groups of children who needed the same next step. Everyone had to be challenged - there was no room to say, "They've done everything." It also meant that the activities undertaken were given the smallest space on the feedback and planning sheet. This is right, the activity is the least important; it's planning the learning that trumps all.

So, our Ofsted target action was met, responsive teaching was born, and Key Stages 1 and 2 were brought in line with early years foundation stage (EYFS) practice, which has always run on these principles. Job's a good 'un.

Tom: Over the last few years, our planning format has changed considerably. We have evolved from using weekly plans, which were not responsive at all, to

11 Clare Sealy, Confessions of a primary headteacher: why my school banned marking and the policy that replaced it, *Third Space Learning* [blog] (26 March 2019). Available at: https://thirdspacelearning.com/blog/why-my-school-banned-marking-confessions-of-a-primary-headteacher/.

using a five-minute lesson plan.[12] This gave us the opportunity to include feedback from our lessons. Both these planning formats worked well in terms of planning the activities for the children to complete. However, what they lacked was a clear understanding of where each child was in their learning and what needed to happen in order for each child to progress. Since moving to our new whole-class feedback model, this has improved dramatically. Although there are no more physical marks in the children's books, each child is catered for in the planning, which means lessons are more focused on each and every child's personal learning and progress. At first, conciseness was challenging: it was difficult to resist giving each child an individual comment. A year down the line, it is much easier to group children by their needs and plan their next steps to aid their progression. This also ensures that groups are flexible and prevents children being typecast. Personally, I find this format works really well in the core subjects as there is clear progression from lesson to lesson. For foundation subjects, where the flow is less apparent, this is slightly trickier. However, my colleagues seem to share my positive opinion, and the time-saving element has been fantastic for my work–life balance.

Takeaway points:

- Feedback doesn't need to involve written comments in books – in fact, feedback may well be invisible to the pupil.
- We need to ask the question, "How is the work I am seeing today going to inform my teaching of this class tomorrow?"
- Changing our understanding of feedback not only leads to more effective teaching but to more efficient teaching as well.

12 The five-minute lesson plan, originally developed by Shaun Allison, used by Ashdown Primary School involves recording the misconceptions and errors picked up from the work of the previous lesson and the plans on how to address them in the following lesson. You can find templates of Ross Morrison McGill's version of the five-minute lesson plan at: https://www.teachertoolkit.co.uk/5minplan/.

LEAD LIKE NOBODY'S WATCHING

Poor school leadership seems to come from the same place as poor teaching. It is fear of an outside observer that is driving poor decisions. Fear of Ofsted, MAT inspections or the reaction of parents pushes leaders to move away from decisions that would be in the best interest of their pupils to ones that are about papering over cracks and putting on a brave face. In the long term, no one wins from such an approach. These problems are tightly linked to deep systemic problems in education that are far beyond the remit of this book to unpick. Luckily, within our education system we have many brave leaders who are determined to do their best for their pupils. In each of these case studies you can see one thing in common: these leaders allow teachers to get on and teach, free of the complications that make teaching less effective and efficient.

CONCLUSION

Let us finish by considering two characters from Greek mythology. The first, Prometheus, engaged in a bit of petty larceny and stole fire from the gods to help his fellow man. His punishment for this light-fingered approach to altruism? To be tied to a rock for all eternity whilst a bird arrived daily to peck out his liver. The second, Sisyphus, tyrant king of Corinth who defied the gods, took Death captive and tricked his grieving widow, all in an attempt to gain immortality. His punishment for his many crimes? To push a rock up a hill, repeatedly and endlessly. No liver-pecking required.

On the face of it, it would seem that Prometheus got the worse deal, but I would suggest that the ancient Greeks knew a thing or two about punishment and, sadly, about teaching in the 21st century. Sisyphus' punishment was a cruel psychological torture. He was pushing a weight up a hill with no end in sight; as he thought he was about to finish, the rock would roll back down again and he would have to start from the beginning. He had no motivation to keep pushing, other than the fear of being crushed by the weight if he stopped, he had no control over this task and knew that it was essentially pointless. Do you see where I am going with this?

I am worried that we have made teaching a Sisyphean task. We have given teachers an unmanageable workload and removed their agency to make decisions about it. We recognise that much of what we are asked to do is pointless but fear that if we stop, we'll get crushed.

What is worse is that we have, at times, abetted this torture. Too many of us bought into the myth of martyrdom and joined in with the humblebrag about how much marking we have to do at the weekend or just how much time we spent triple mounting work for the display board. We allowed an image of nobility to surround the teacher who sacrificed their time "for the kids" and wore their exhaustion like a badge of honour. At the same time, we witnessed a characterisation of "lazy" teachers who shuffled into work unprepared, moaned in the staffroom and were first in their cars when the bell went.

I really hope that this book has shown that there is another way: that we can avoid teacher burnout by focusing on the simple things that are efficient and embracing the complexities that make them work, all whilst avoiding the complications that add to our workload without doing anything to improve the education of our pupils. If we return to the introduction, we find Daniel Muijs' analogy of teachers being asked to eat their soup with a fork and getting on with it despite the increased time, demands and mess it creates. We really can just insist on a spoon.

In researching this book, I was heartened by the number of schools out there who are already empowering teachers to teach like nobody's watching. I am lucky enough to work in such a school myself and can appreciate the enormous difference it makes to work within a culture of professional trust. However, I have worked in very different schools over the years, including ones in which it felt like I was battling the prevailing culture.

If you work in such a school, know that it is a battle you can win. I hope that this book has given you some of the strategies you will need to close your classroom door and just get on and teach, leaving the non-negotiables and shiny-suited assistant head teacher initiatives outside. If you get tired of the fight, then please know that there are schools doing things in other ways. What we don't need - and can't afford - are more brilliant teachers being driven out of the profession, crushed by the Sisyphean rock.

So, I urge you, step away from the rock, throw away the fork that is thrust upon you and grab your own spoon. It is time we all taught like nobody's watching.

BIBLIOGRAPHY

Abel, Magdalena and Henry L. Roediger, III (2018) The testing effect in a social setting: does retrieval practice benefit a listener?, *Journal of Experimental Psychology: Applied* 24(3): 347–359.

Allen, Becky (2018) What if we cannot measure pupil progress? *Becky Allen* [blog] (23 May). Available at: https://rebeccaallen.co.uk/2018/05/23/what-if-we-cannot-measure-pupil-progress/.

Allen, Becky (2019) Writing the rules of the grading game (part I): the grade changes the child, *Becky Allen [blog]* (24 April). Available at: https://rebeccaallen.co.uk/2019/04/24/grading-game-part-i/.

Allen, Rebecca and Sam Sims (2018) *The Teacher Gap* (Abingdon: Routledge).

Allison, Shaun and Andy Tharby (2015) *Making Every Lesson Count: Six Principles to Support Great Teaching and Learning* (Carmarthen: Crown House Publishing).

Allison, Shaun (2018) Supporting retrieval practice with Cornell note taking, *Class Teaching* [blog] (24 September). Available at: https://classteaching.wordpress.com/2018/09/24/supporting-retrieval-practice-with-cornell-note-taking/.

Baird, Jo-Anne, David Andrich, Therese Hopfenbeck and Gordon Stobart (2017) Assessment and learning: fields apart?, *Assessment in Education: Principles, Policy and Practice* 24(3): 317–350.

Berger, Ron (2003) *An Ethic of Excellence: Building a Culture of Craftsmanship with Students* (Portsmouth, NH: Heinemann).

Berliner, David (2001) Learning about and learning from expert teachers, *International Journal of Educational Research* 35: 463–482.

Berliner, David (2004) Expert teachers: their characteristics, development and accomplishments. In I. Batllori, R. Obiols, A. E. Gomez Martinez, M. Oller, I. Freixa, J. Pages and I. Blanch (eds), *De la teoria… a l'aula: Formacio del professorat ensenyament de las ciències socials* (Barcelona: Departament de Didàctica de la Llengua i la Literatura, i de les Ciències Socials, Universitat Autònoma de Barcelona), pp. 13–28. Available at: https://www.researchgate.net/profile/David_Berliner2/publication/255666969_Expert_Teachers_Their_Characteristics_Development_and_Accomplishments/links/02e7e53c6d5e6b68d7000000/Expert-Teachers-Their-Characteristics-Development-and-Accomplishments.pdf.

Bjork, Robert A. (1994) Memory and metamemory considerations in the training of human beings. In Janet Metcalfe and Arthur P. Shimamura (eds), *Metacognition: Knowing About Knowing* (Cambridge, MA: MIT Press),pp. 185–215.

Bjork, Elizabeth Ligon and Robert A. Bjork (2003) Intentional forgetting can increase, not decrease, residual influences of to-be-forgotten information, *Journal of Experimental Psychology: Learning, Memory, and Cognition* 29(4): 524–531.

Bjork, Elizabeth L. and Robert Bjork (2011) Making things hard on yourself, but in a good way: creating desirable difficulties to enhance learning. In Morton A. Gernsbacher, Richard W. Pew,

Leaetta M. Hough and James Pomerantz (eds), *Psychology and the Real World: Essays Illustrating Fundamental Contributions to Society*, 2nd edn (New York: Worth Publishers), pp. 56-64.

Bjork, Elizabeth Ligon, Jeri L. Little and Benjamin C. Storm (2014) Multiple-choice testing as a desirable difficulty in the classroom, *Journal of Applied Research in Memory and Cognition* 3(3): 165–170.

Bourdieu, Pierre (2018 [1973]) Cultural reproduction and social reproduction. In Richard Brown (ed.), *Knowledge, Education and Cultural Change* (Abingdon: Routledge), pp. 71–112.

Boxer, Adam (2019) What is the best way to motivate students in your subject?, *Impact: Journal of the Chartered College of Teaching* 5: 10–11.

Butler, Andrew C. and Henry L. Roediger, III (2008) Feedback enhances the positive effects and reduces the negative effects of multiple-choice testing, *Memory and Cognition* 36(3): 604–616.

Butler, Ruth (1988) Enhancing and undermining intrinsic motivation: the effect of task-involving and ego-involving evaluation on interest and performance, *British Journal of Educational Psychology* 58(1): 1–14.

Catling, Simon, Rachel Bowles, John Halocha, Fran Martin and Steve Rawlinson (2007) The state of geography in English primary schools, *Geography* 92(2): 118–136.

Christodoulou, Daisy (2014) *Seven Myths About Education* (Abingdon: Routledge).

Christodoulou, Daisy (2017) *Making Good Progress: The Future of Assessment for Learning* (Oxford: Oxford University Press).

Christodoulou, Daisy (2018) Could handwriting bias write off exam chances?, *TES* (23 October). Available at: https://www.tes.com/news/could-handwriting-bias-write-exam-chances.

Clark, Christina and Jonathan Douglas (2011) *Young People's Reading and Writing: An In-Depth Study Focusing on Enjoyment, Behaviour, Attitudes and Attainment* (London: National Literacy Trust). Available at: https://files.eric.ed.gov/fulltext/ED521656.pdf.

Coe, Robert (2013) Improving Education: A Triumph of Hope over Experience, Inaugural Lecture of Professor Robert Coe, Durham University (18 June). Available at: http://www.cem.org/attachments/publications/ImprovingEducation2013.pdf.

Coe, Robert (2018) But that is NOT AN ASSESSMENT, *CEMblog* [blog] (20 June). Available at: http://www.cem.org/blog/but-that-is-not-an-assessment/.

Coe, Robert, Cesare Aloisi, Steve Higgins and Lee Elliot Major (2014) *What Makes Great Teaching? Review of the Underpinning Research* (London: Sutton Trust). Available at: https://www.suttontrust.com/wp-content/uploads/2014/10/What-makes-great-teaching-FINAL-4.11.14-1.pdf.

Collier, Hatty (2016) Teachers "opting to work part-time to finish marking on days off", *Evening Standard* (3 April). Available at: http://www.standard.co.uk/news/education/teachers-opting-to-work-parttime-to-finish-marking-on-days-off-a3506086.html.

Counsell, Christine (2018) Taking curriculum seriously, *Impact: Journal of the Chartered College of Teaching* (September). Available at: https://impact.chartered.college/article/taking-curriculum-seriously/.

Cowan, Nelson (2010) The magical mystery four: how is working memory capacity limited, and why?, *Current Directions in Psychological Science* 19(1): 51–57.

Daulby, Jules (2018) All hail! In the inclusive classroom, the mini whiteboard is queen, *Jules Daulby* [blog] (9 December) Available at: https://julesdaulby.com/2018/12/09/all-hail-in-the-inclusive-classroom-the-mini-whiteboard-is-queen/.

Department for Education (2016) *Eliminating Unnecessary Workload Around Marking: Report of the Independent Teacher Workload Review Group* (March). Available at: https://www.gov.uk/government/publications/reducing-teacher-workload-marking-policy-review-group-report.

Didau, David (2015) *What If Everything You Knew About Education Was Wrong?* (Carmarthen: Crown House Publishing).

Didau, David (2019) *Making Kids Cleverer: A Manifesto for Closing the Advantage Gap* (Carmarthen, Crown House Publishing).

Didau, David and Pedro de Bruyckere (2017) Learning myths. In Carl Hendrick and Robin Macpherson (eds), *What Does This Look Like in the Classroom? Bridging the Gap Between Research and Practice* (Woodbridge: John Catt Educational).

Didau, David and Nick Rose (2016) *What Every Teacher Needs to Know About Psychology* (Woodbridge: John Catt Educational).

Ebbinghaus, Hermann (1913 [1885]) *Memory: A Contribution to Experimental Psychology*, trs Henry A. Ruger and Clara E. Bussenius (New York: Teachers College, Columbia University).

Egan, Kieran (2002) *Getting It Wrong from the Beginning: Our Progressivist Inheritance from Herbert Spencer, John Dewey, and Jean Piaget* (New Haven and London: Yale University Press).

Engelmann, Siegfried, Wesley C. Becker, Douglas Carnine and Russell Gersten (1988) The direct instruction follow through model: design and outcomes, *Education and Treatment of Children* 11(4): 303–317.

Enser, Mark (2017) What makes effective learning?, *Heathfield Teach Share* [blog] (19 May). Available at: https://heathfieldteachshare.wordpress.com/2017/05/19/what-makes-effective-learning/.

Enser, Mark (2019) Interleaving: are we getting it all wrong?, *TES* (27 February). Available at: https://www.tes.com/news/interleaving-are-we-getting-it-all-wrong.

Enser, Mark (2019) *Making Every Geography Lesson Count: Six Principles to Support Great Geography Teaching* (Carmarthen: Crown House Publishing).

Firth, Roger (2018) Recontextualising geography as a school subject. In Mark Jones and David Lambert (eds), *Debates in Geography Education*, 2nd edn (Abingdon: Routledge), pp. 275–286.

Ford, Alex (2019) Examinations: the gilded age, *And All That* [blog] (7 March). Available at: http://www.andallthat.co.uk/blog/examinations-the-gilded-age.

Gathercole, Susan E. and Tracy Packiam Alloway (2007) *Understanding Working Memory: A Classroom Guide* (London: Harcourt Assessment). Available at: https://www.mrc-cbu.cam.ac.uk/wp-content/uploads/2013/01/WM-classroom-guide.pdf.

Hattie, John and Helen Timperley (2007) The power of feedback, *Review of Educational Research* 77(1): 81–112.

Hazel, Will (2018) Reasons to worry: 5 new facts about teacher retention, *TES* (27 September). Available at: https://www.tes.com/news/reasons-worry-5-new-facts-about-teacher-retention.

Hendrick, Carl (2017) Designing a super-curriculum, *Wellington Learning and Research Centre* [blog] (21 February). Available at: https://learning.wellingtoncollege.org.uk/designing-a-super-curriculum/.

Hirsch, Jr., Eric Donald (1987) *Cultural Literacy: What Every American Needs to Know* (Boston, MA: Houghton Mifflin).

Kahn, Barbara E. and Brian Wansink (2004) The influence of assortment structure on perceived variety and consumption quantities, *Journal of Consumer Research* 30(4): 519–533.

Karpicke, Jeffrey D. and Phillip J. Grimaldi (2012) Retrieval-based learning: a perspective for enhancing meaningful learning, *Educational Psychology Review* 24: 401–418.

Kirschner, Paul A., John Sweller and Richard E. Clark (2006) Why minimal guidance during instruction does not work: an analysis of the failure of constructivist, discovery, project-based, experiential, and inquiry-based teaching, *Educational Psychologist* 41(2): 75–86.

Knight, Oliver and David Benson (2014) *Creating Outstanding Classrooms: A Whole-School Approach* (Abingdon: Routledge).

Kruger, Justin and David Dunning (1999) Unskilled and unaware of it: how difficulties in recognizing one's own incompetence lead to inflated self-assessments, *Journal of Personality and Social Psychology* 77(6): 1121–1134.

Lightfoot, Liz (2016) Nearly half of England's teachers plan to leave in next five years, *The Guardian* (22 March). Available at: https://www.theguardian.com/education/2016/mar/22/teachers-plan-leave-five-years-survey-workload-england.

McAllister, Keith (2010) The ASD Friendly Classroom – Design Complexity, Challenge and Characteristics. Available at: https://www.researchgate.net/profile/Keith_Mcallister/publication/267684638_The_ASD_Friendly_Classroom_-_Design_Complexity_Challenge_and_Characteristics/links/54942cd30cf2e572fa53a8cb/The-ASD-Friendly-Classroom-Design-Complexity-Challenge-and-Characteristics.pdf.

McInerney, Laura (2017) How often are teachers expected to mark work?, *TeacherTapp* [blog] (November 2017). Available at: http://teachertapp.co.uk/2017/11/often-teachers-required-mark-work/.

McInerney, Laura (2018) What teachers tapped this week #50, *TeacherTapp* [blog] (10 September). Available at: http://teachertapp.co.uk/2018/09/what-teachers-tapped-this-week-50-10th-september/.

McInerney, Laura (2018) What teachers tapped this week #56, *TeacherTapp* [blog] (22 October). Available at: http://teachertapp.co.uk/2018/10/what-teachers-tapped-this-week-56-22nd-october-2018/.

McInerney, Laura (2019) Behaviour: what is really going on in schools?, *TeacherTapp* [blog] (10 February). Available at: http://teachertapp.co.uk/2019/02/behaviour-what-is-really-going-on-in-schools-2019/.

Macpherson, Robin (2017) Designing a super-curriculum, Wellington Learning and Research Centre [blog] (21 February). Available at: https://learning.wellingtoncollege.org.uk/designing-a-super-curriculum/.

Mayer, Richard E. and Richard B. Anderson (1991) Animations need narrations: an experimental test of a dual-coding hypothesis, *Journal of Educational Psychology* 83(4): 484–490.

Meyer, Jan H. F. and Ray Land (2003) Threshold concepts and troublesome knowledge: linkages to ways of thinking and practising within the disciplines. In Chris Rust (ed.), *Improving Student Learning: Theory and Practice Ten Years On* (Oxford: Oxford Centre for Staff and Learning Development), pp. 412–424.

Muijs, Daniel (2018) Keynote address at the researchEd Durrington conference, Durrington High School (28 April).

Murre, Jaap J. M. and Joeri Dros (2015) Replication and analysis of Ebbinghaus' forgetting curve, *PLoS ONE* 10(7): e0120644. Available at: https://doi.org/10.1371/journal.pone.0120644.

Myatt, Mary (2018) *The Curriculum: Gallimaufry to Coherence* (Woodbridge: John Catt Educational).

Nuthall, Graham (2007) *The Hidden Lives of Learners* (Wellington: NZCER Press).

Ofsted (2015) *Key Stage 3: The Wasted Years?* Ref: 150106 (September). Available at: https://www.gov.uk/government/publications/key-stage-3-the-wasted-years.

Ofsted (2018) Ofsted Inspection – Clarification for Schools (guidance to accompany *School Inspection Handbook*. Ref: 150066, September). Available at: https://www.gov.uk/government/publications/school-inspection-handbook-from-september-2015.

Paivio, Allan (1991) Dual coding theory: retrospect and current status, *Canadian Journal of Psychology* 45(3): 255–287.

Priory, James (2018) What is the super curriculum?, *School House*. Available at: https://www.schoolhousemagazine.co.uk/education/what-is-the-super-curriculum/.

Roche, Fergal (2017) *Mining for Gold: Stories of Effective Teachers* (Woodbridge: John Catt Educational).

Roediger, III, Henry L. and Jeffrey D. Karpicke (2006) Test-enhanced learning: taking memory tests improves long-term retention, *Psychological Science* 17(3): 249–255.

Roediger, III, Henry L., Adam L. Putnam and Megan A. Smith (2011) Ten benefits of testing and their applications to educational practice. In Jose P. Mestre and Brian H. Ross (eds), *The Psychology of Learning and Motivation. Vol. 55: Cognition in Education* (San Diego, CA: Elsevier Academic Press), pp. 1-36.

Rosenshine, Barak (2012) Principles of instruction: research-based strategies that all teachers should know, *American Educator* 36(1): 12–19, 39. Available at: https://www.aft.org/sites/default/files/periodicals/Rosenshine.pdf.

Schwerdt, Guido and Amelie C. Wuppermann (2009) Is Traditional Teaching Really All That Bad? A Within-Student Between-Subject Approach (April). CESifo Working Paper Series No. 2634. Available at: https://ssrn.com/abstract=1396620.

Sealy, Clare (2019) Confessions of a primary headteacher: why my school banned marking and the policy that replaced it, *Third Space Learning* [blog] (26 March). Available at: https://thirdspacelearning.com/blog/why-my-school-banned-marking-confessions-of-a-primary-headteacher/.

Singh, Anne-Marie, Nadine Marcus and Paul Ayres (2012) The transient information effect: investigating the impact of segmentation on spoken and written text, *Applied Cognitive Psychology* 26(6): 848–853.

Slavin, Robert E. (1980) Cooperative learning, *Review of Educational Research* 50(2): 315–342.

Soderstrom, Nicholas C. and Robert A. Bjork (2015) Learning versus performance: an integrative review, *Perspectives on Psychological Science* 10(2): 176–199.

Spielman, Amanda (2018) HMCI commentary: curriculum and the new education inspection framework (18 September). Available at: https://www.gov.uk/government/speeches/hmci-commentary-curriculum-and-the-new-education-inspection-framework.

Sweller, John (1988) Cognitive load during problem solving: effects on learning, *Cognitive Science* 12(2): 257–285.

Sweller, John (2010) Element interactivity and intrinsic, extraneous, and germane cognitive load, *Educational Psychology Review* 22(2): 123–138.

Sweller, John, Jeroen J. G. van Merrienboer and Fred G. W. C. Paas (1998) Cognitive architecture and instructional design, *Educational Psychology Review* 10(3): 251–296.

Thalheimer, Will (2015) Mythical retention data and the corrupted cone, *Work-Learning Research* [blog] (5 January). Available at: https://www.worklearning.com/2015/01/05/mythical-retention-data-the-corrupted-cone/.

Tickle, Louise (2018) "Every lesson is a battle": why teachers are lining up to leave, *The Guardian* (10 April). Available at: https://www.theguardian.com/education/2018/apr/10/lesson-battle-why-teachers-lining-up-leave.

Treadaway, Mike (2015) Why measuring pupil progress involves more than taking a straight line, *FFT Education Datalab* [blog] (5 March). Available at: https://ffteducationdatalab.org.uk/2015/03/why-measuring-pupil-progress-involves-more-than-taking-a-straight-line/.

Weale, Sally (2017) Teachers must ditch the "neuromyth" of learning styles, say scientists, *The Guardian* (13 March). Available at: https://www.theguardian.com/education/2017/mar/13/teachers-neuromyth-learning-styles-scientists-neuroscience-education.

Willingham, Daniel T. (2004) Ask the cognitive scientist: the privileged status of story, *American Educator* (summer). Available at: https://www.aft.org/periodical/american-educator/summer-2004/ask-cognitive-scientist.

Willingham, Daniel T. (2009) *Why Don't Students Like School? A Cognitive Scientist Answers Questions About How the Mind Works and What It Means for the Classroom* (San Francisco, CA: Jossey-Bass).

Willingham, Daniel (2012) School time, knowledge, and reading comprehension, *Daniel Willingham - Science and Education* [blog] (7 March). Available at: http://www.danielwillingham.com/daniel-willingham-science-and-education-blog/school-time-knowledge-and-reading-comprehension.

Young, Michael (2007) *Bringing Knowledge Back In: From Social Constructivism to Social Realism in the Sociology of Education* (Abingdon: Routledge).

INDEX

Mark Enser is Head of Geography and Research Lead at Heathfield Community College, East Sussex, and has been teaching for over a decade in a wide range of schools. He is also a *TES* columnist and regular conference speaker, and is the author of *Making Every Geography Lesson Count*. He blogs at teachreal.wordpress.com.

What is left of his free time is spent running up hills or recovering with a cup of coffee.

Follow him on Twitter @EnserMark